# CBT WORKBOOK FOR KIDS

# CBT

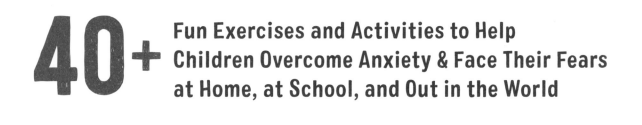

## WORKBOOK for KIDS

**40+** Fun Exercises and Activities to Help
Children Overcome Anxiety & Face Their Fears
at Home, at School, and Out in the World

## BY HEATHER DAVIDSON, Psy.D, BCN

Illustrations by Sarah Rebar

callisto
publishing
an imprint of Sourcebooks

For Mom.

For Robb.

For all of my kiddos and their families—past, present, and future.

Published by Callisto Publishing LLC C/O Sourcebooks LLC
P.O. Box 4410, Naperville, Illinois 60567-4410
(630) 961-3900
callistopublishing.com

This product conforms to all applicable CPSC and CPSIA standards.

Source of Production: Wing King Tong Paper Products Co.Ltd. Shenzhen, Guangdong Province, China
Date of Production: September 2023
Run Number: 5034647

Printed and bound in China.
WKT 2

# Table of Contents

· · · · · · · · · · · · · · · · · · · · · · · · · · · · · · ·

# A LETTER TO
# GROWN-UPS

• • • • • • • • • • • • • • • • • • • • • • • • • • • • • • • • • •

**DO YOU THINK YOU HAVE AN ANXIOUS CHILD?** Whether you're still figuring out if they're within the "normal" range, or you already know anxiety is one of your child's biggest struggles; whether your child just developed anxiety, or they've had it for years—this workbook can help. I designed it so you and your child can better manage anxiety and take back control of your lives. The strategies I've chosen work, whatever the level of your child's anxiety. Cognitive behavioral therapy (CBT) is a scientifically proven intervention that helps kids overcome their anxiety symptoms. CBT interventions target thoughts and perception (the cognitive part), and responses and actions (the behavior part). It works to change your child's pattern of anxiety-driven thoughts and provides them with behavioral strategies to engage with life and do the things they want to do, regardless of how anxious they may be feeling.

This book addresses a wide range of anxiety symptoms: generalized anxiety, panic, specific phobias, and even some obsessive thoughts. It will teach your child the skills they need to stop avoiding things that make them anxious and live happier, healthier lives. Although this book is designed for your child, *you* are a critical part in their successfully overcoming their anxiety. Depending on their age and reading level, you may need to stick close by to guide them the first several times they do the exercises.

Before you introduce this book to your child, please read the Just for Parents section (page 108) to understand your role in helping them learn to manage their symptoms. You may need to change some things about your own behavior in order to maximize your child's success, and that section explains what this means and what you can do.

If your child has an acute problem right now, like school anxiety and refusal, you can flip straight to the relevant section. Otherwise, plan to work straight through the book in order. Every family is different, so go at a pace that works best for you and your child, but you will maximize the benefits to your whole family by eventually working through every exercise in the book.

Remember, these skills and strategies are scientifically proven to work—if you practice them, you'll see results. Parenting a child who suffers from anxiety can be tough, but your dedication and these techniques are everything you and your child need to succeed. You've got this!

# A LETTER TO
# KIDS

· · · · · · · · · · · · · · · · · · · · · · · · · · · · · · · · · · · · ·

**THIS BOOK IS FOR YOU!** Do you ever feel like anxiety is taking over your life? It can cause problems at home and at school and make things that should be fun—like sleepovers or going to the movies—scary and UN-fun. Worst of all, it's hard to explain how you feel and why you don't want to do the things you used to like. Here's the truth: Every single one of us feels anxious sometimes. Feeling anxiety doesn't mean there's anything wrong with you. Sometimes anxiety can take control, but this book will show you how to put anxiety back in its place, so it's not the boss of you anymore.

# CHAPTER 1:

# WHAT IS ANXIETY, ANYWAY?

# HOW DOES ANXIETY MAKE YOU FEEL?

What is "anxiety," anyway? Maybe you've heard the word on TV or heard one of your parents say it. Maybe once a friend said they were feeling anxious, and you were too embarrassed to ask what they meant. If you don't know exactly what anxiety means, you're not the only one! Lots of people use the word—even some grown-ups—but many of us don't know the true meaning.

Anxiety is a lot like another word: *worry*. Both worry and anxiety describe nervous or scared feelings. How can you tell the difference between the two? Well, worry is usually in our thoughts and is specific—you worry *about* something, like a hard test—and anxiety is something you may feel all the time, that sometimes has physical symptoms like a racing heart, and that you can feel for no particular reason at all.

Think about it this way: It's usually easy to explain what you're *worried* about (like a big test), but it can be hard to explain why you feel *anxious*—like the knot in your stomach or the racing heart you may get just from going to school. Because worry has a reason, it's easier to explain with words, but it's hard to explain your anxiety because you may not be sure why you're feeling it.

Although anxiety and worry often feel bad, they can be very useful feelings. Sometimes being worried helps us get a project finished or makes us do the best job we can. Without worrying about doing a good job on our project, or staying strong and healthy, we wouldn't care too much about going to school or eating healthy food. Sometimes, worry can act as an alarm and help keep us safe. We certainly wouldn't want to completely get rid of anxiety and worry—these feelings can be a healthy part of all the emotions we feel.

We have so many different emotions running around inside us it's sometimes hard to tell them apart. For example, when you're really upset, it can be hard to tell if you're angry or sad. In the same way, sometimes it's difficult to know when one emotion, out of the many we feel, is causing us *lots* of problems. Here's a story about different emotions:

Maya is worried about her relationship with her friends. She's not sure if they like spending time with her, and she's scared they might decide they don't want to be friends anymore. Maya's worry turns into anxiety—whenever she is with her friends, her heart beats very fast and her hands get all sweaty. After she feels anxious for many days in a row, she begins to feel angry with her friends—she wonders why they don't like her and what makes them so much better. These thoughts make Maya feel guilty because she doesn't want to think badly of her friends. This guilt then leads right back to anxiety, which then leads to Maya wanting to avoid her friends completely. Maya thinks that if she avoids her friends, maybe she can avoid feeling all those horrible feelings.

Can you see how we can feel many emotions, all starting from one anxious or worried thought? Sometimes you can feel two, three, four emotions all at once. Sometimes one emotion leads to another emotion, which can lead to another then another . . .

Think about the first time you went to school, or went to a sleepover, or had to give a class presentation. Remember how that felt? Maybe your heart started to race really fast, or your hands felt all sticky. Or maybe you felt like it was hard to breathe, or that you were about to cry. These are all ways your body lets you know you feel nervous or scared.

Let's learn more about your anxious thoughts and feelings. You're going to do a few exercises to help you figure out when you feel anxious and what types of thoughts and physical sensations you experience when you do.

# I Feel Anxious When . . .

| | NO, NEVER | WELL, SOMETIMES | YES, ALL THE TIME! |
|---|---|---|---|
| I'm alone | | | |
| I get a bad grade | | | |
| I have a fight with my friend | | | |
| I have a fight with my parents | | | |
| I'm in the dark | | | |
| I'm doing my homework | | | |
| I don't feel well physically | | | |
| I'm outside | | | |
| I have a cold | | | |
| I'm thinking about getting sick | | | |
| I go somewhere new | | | |
| I'm with new people | | | |
| I don't know what makes me anxious | | | |

Use your checkmarks from the table to answer the following questions. If you can think of something else not on the checklist that makes you anxious, make sure you write it down. Figuring out what makes you anxious is the first step in overcoming it.

**My anxiety is high when I**_____

_____

_____

**My anxiety is medium when I**_____

_____

_____

**My anxiety is low when I**_____

_____

_____

# When I'm Anxious, I . . .

We can feel anxiety in many different ways. Just like we wanted to find out *what* makes you anxious, we also want to find out what *happens* when you get anxious. What do you do when you get anxious? How does your body feel? Circle what happens to you.

## FEEL . . .

racing heartbeat

sweaty hands

teary eyes

headache

stomachache

tight muscles

shakiness

fast breathing

feeling dizzy

feeling tingly

sweaty all over

shivering

nauseous

## THINK . . .

about it over and over

the WORST will happen

confused thoughts

negative thoughts

overwhelmed thoughts

angry thoughts

sad thoughts

I need help

I can't do anything

there is something wrong with me

I'm not as good as others

I need to hide

I can't think

# WORRIES BIG AND SMALL

Now that you know a little more about anxiety and worry, let's focus on the "worry" part and learn about all the different kinds of worry we can feel. Some worries are big and some are small; what's the difference? What makes some worries big and loud instead of small and quiet?

Think about your worries like rubber balls bouncing around in your head. You don't mind—or even notice much—a small ball bouncing just a little. But when a great big ball starts bouncing a lot and you can't make it stop, it feels uncomfortable and distracts you from important things like talking to your friends or paying attention in class.

A bouncy ball can't bounce if we don't make it bounce. While we can't make the ball magically disappear, it also won't magically bounce on its own! You have to pick it up and *make it* bounce. The same is true of worries. If you don't pay attention to your worries, they don't magically disappear, but they also don't keep bouncing around in your head.

Maybe your biggest worry is being alone and you think it would be *very* scary to be by yourself—this is like a big bounce in your head. Then you worry that anytime you're alone, something bad could happen—*boing*—there's another big, noisy bounce! It might be hard to have fun playing, or fall asleep, or do anything at all with all that bouncing. But if you don't pay attention to those bouncy balls, they won't bounce as much. Together, we're going to learn how to take your big, loud worries and make them small and quiet, so you can keep doing all the things you want to do.

# ANXIETY'S NOT THE BOSS OF YOU

Feeling anxiety is completely, totally normal. Every person in the world gets anxious now and then. It's just part of life, and feeling anxious and worried sometimes can help keep us safe—like when we look both ways before we cross the street because we're worried about cars. But for some people, worry and anxiety can start to get out of hand. When you start worrying about things that aren't really scary, or you stop doing things you like because your anxiety tells you they aren't safe, anxiety is starting to be the boss of you. That doesn't feel good, and it can cause you to miss out on all kinds of good things.

The good news is, you can learn to feel more comfortable with your healthy anxiety (the kind that keeps you safe) and accept that some anxiety is just going to happen. Plus, you can make sure the anxiety you do feel knows who the real boss is: YOU!

Does your anxiety ever try to be your boss? Do your worried thoughts ever tell you that you shouldn't go to the store with your parents, or sleep over at a friend's house because something bad might happen? Sometimes anxiety thinks it knows best, and it tries to tell you what to do, where to go, and how to feel. But anxiety usually thinks things are a lot scarier than they really are. It's trying to keep us safe and happy, but when it gets out of hand, when those balls start bouncing around too much, anxiety makes things worse for us, not better.

So, how can you tell anxiety it's not going to be the boss of you anymore? Right now, that might sound impossible. It's okay to feel confused or nervous about becoming your own boss again, but there are lots of things you can do to stop anxiety from taking over your life.

First of all, it's important to learn how and when to say no to your anxiety, so you can keep doing the things you love to do—like going to parties—and also the things you need to do—like going to school. One thing we know about kids whose anxiety gets out of hand is that their worried thoughts sometimes tell them school is *dangerous*. What would you do if you thought that? You'd probably do whatever you could to stay home where you feel safe.

The problem is that school can be really great—it's where you learn, see your friends, play games, and grow. But if anxiety were your boss, you'd probably feel like you had to listen to it, even when it told you to do things you didn't want to do, or miss out on things you love. One way to start making your own choices again is to stand up to anxiety when it tells you something is too scary to do—after all, just because someone tells you something, doesn't mean you have to believe it.

Imagination—which is usually a good thing—can team up with anxiety and make everything seem worse. Your imagination is great for playing pretend and making things exciting, but it can also make your anxiety feel bigger, stronger, and way more real than it actually is. Thinking that school is scary is bad enough, and if your imagination runs wild, you may see all the scary things that could happen playing in your head like a movie. But if you remember that you're *imagining* all those dangers, your imagination could go back to helping you have fun instead of helping anxiety boss you around.

In this exercise, circle the things your anxiety tells you aren't safe, then we'll find some ways you can calm down and feel better.

# Things My Anxiety Tells Me Aren't Safe

Here is a list of some common things that anxiety may tell you are more dangerous than they really are.

- Being alone
- Loud noises
- Weird smells
- Dogs
- School
- Heights
- Cars

- Trains
- Planes
- Homework
- Storms
- Tests
- Movies
- Darkness

- Germs
- Being sick
- Getting hurt
- Strangers
- Teachers
- Yelling

Now, in the circles, draw the ones that are the scariest to you.

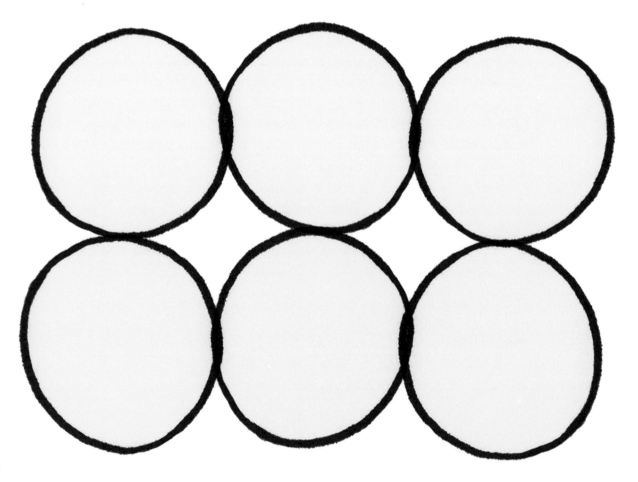

# Belly Breathing

Did you know that when you take big breaths into and out of your stomach, it can make you feel calm? You'll need to make sure that when you take that big breath in, your stomach gets big and full of air, and when you breathe out, your stomach falls and releases all that air. Those big breaths put you in a state where you can easily show anxiety who's boss. Follow the steps to learn how to do this.

**STEP 1**

Lie down on a couch, your bed, or even the floor.

**STEP 5**

Repeat steps 3 and 4 a few more times. Are you feeling a little calmer?

**STEP 2**

Place a stuffed animal, toy, balloon, or your own hand on your stomach.

**STEP 4**

Take one big breath OUT while counting to four, making sure that you pull your stomach in enough to make whatever is on your stomach move DOWN.

**STEP 3**

Take one big breath IN while counting to three, making sure that you push your stomach out enough to make whatever is on your stomach move UP.

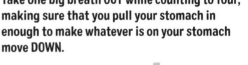

# Word-Search Puzzle

There are lots more things you can do to feel calmer. Here is a word search with words that can help you overcome your anxiety. To make it fun, some words go across the page and some down the page.

```
M  U  S  I  C  F  G  W  R  Y
O  F  D  S  W  D  A  D  V  B
M  R  T  Y  E  R  R  W  Q  Z
D  J  O  U  R  N  A  L  D  R
W  Q  B  F  R  I  E  N  D  S
V  B  N  C  E  R  G  T  F  I
D  W  R  I  T  E  W  E  T  N
T  Y  U  D  R  A  W  G  R  G
```

Answers: MUSIC, JOURNAL, FRIENDS, WRITE, DRAW, MOM, SING

# Breathe the Rainbow

Now take those deep-breathing skills and breathe the rainbow! When you take your big breaths in and out, think about your favorite thing that matches each color.

| |
|---|
| **Red fire trucks, apples, hearts, strawberries, roses** |
| **Lions, pumpkins, basketballs, goldfish** |
| Sunshine, rubber duckies, bananas, sunflowers |
| Frogs, trees, four-leaf clovers, dinosaurs, aliens |
| Blueberries, balloons, bluebirds, Smurfs, Cookie Monster |
| **Grapes, lilacs, butterflies, popsicles** |

CHAPTER 2:

# WHAT CAN YOU DO ABOUT ANXIETY?

# TRIANGLES AND OTHER SHAPES

Define anxiety: check! You've taken your first step to taking back power from your anxiety. But now that you understand what anxiety is, what can you *do* about it? The first thing to do is to better understand how anxiety is created, along with all its different signs and symptoms, like sweaty palms and scary thoughts. The best way to understand how anxiety is created is by . . . (drum-roll, please) looking at a triangle!

That may sound kind of weird, but it turns out the triangle is a great way to visualize how all our feelings, including anxiety, are connected to one another.

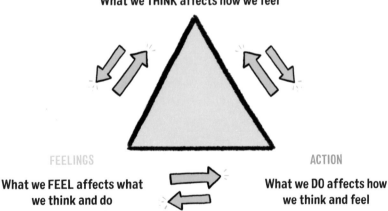

**THOUGHTS**

**What we THINK affects how we feel**

**FEELINGS**

**What we FEEL affects what we think and do**

**ACTION**

**What we DO affects how we think and feel**

Let's break this triangle down and see what it all means. At the top of the triangle are your *thoughts*. This includes everything you think throughout the day. For example: Your dad tells you a new babysitter is going to start watching you. You may think "I don't want a new babysitter!" This thought can trigger a specific *feeling*, like fear or frustration. You may feel fearful because the new babysitter is a stranger, or you may feel frustrated because your parents made a decision without telling you. These uncomfortable feelings can then lead you to take a specific *action*. You might yell at your parents or run to your room and slam the door. You may plan your action as a way to communicate your feelings, or your action could be something you didn't realize you were doing until you'd already done it. Oops!

Can you see how the corners of the triangle—thoughts, feelings, and actions—are all connected? Here's another example: Say you get a bad grade on a test you studied really hard for. Feeling sad and disappointed, you might *think*, "I'm never going to do well in school." This unhappy thought could affect how you *feel* and how you *behave* (action). When you have this thought, maybe you feel bad about yourself or feel hopeless about getting better grades. When that happens, you might stop paying attention in class or doing your homework because it seems pointless when you think you're never going to do well in school. See how, again, your thoughts, emotions, and behavior all interact? Every point on that triangle is important.

The triangle isn't the only important shape. Here, the circle represents the big bad loop of anxious thoughts and feelings.

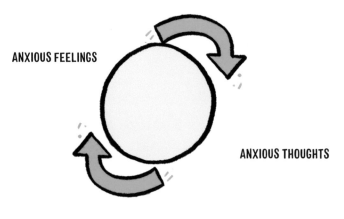

ANXIOUS FEELINGS

ANXIOUS THOUGHTS

This circle is like a bad dream on repeat. Let's use the same example we used for the triangle: You got a bad grade on a test you studied really hard for, and your anxious thought is the same: "I'm never going to do well in school." Once you have that anxious thought and feel really scared, confused, angry, or worried— well, then you have another anxious thought. This next thought is "I'm stupid," which makes you feel even more scared, sad, and worried. Those feelings lead to more anxious thoughts. Do you see how anxious thoughts and feelings feed off each other and create a big, bad, awful circle of unhappy thoughts?

Let's look again at our triangle and our circle. Do you see the arrows in the triangle and circle that show how things move and change? Those arrows are very important and are the first big step in understanding what you can actually do about your anxiety. One arrow connects thoughts with emotions, and the next connects emotions to actions (behaviors), and actions to emotions. That's a lot of connections!

Most people think there is only one connection: The situation they're in is what makes them feel bad emotions. This is a mistake—a mistake kids and adults make every day! It's not the *situation* you're in that causes your emotion; it is actually how you *think* about the situation that causes your emotion. Is that confusing? Let's look at an example.

Kyle got a bad grade on a test he studied really hard for. He feels very worried about how this will affect his overall grade, he feels anxious sensations in his body, and he feels sad that he did not perform better. He feels sad and worried because of the test grade, right? Nope! It is actually Kyle's *thoughts* that make him feel worried and sad. If he thinks "I'm never going to do well in school now" or "I'm stupid," we'd expect that he'd feel lots of big, bad, strong emotions. But if he thinks "That's okay. I'll try harder next time and see if I can change some of my study habits," then maybe he would still feel a little sad, but he certainly wouldn't feel overwhelming sadness or anxiety. Do you see how the situation is the same—Kyle failed a test—but the way he *thinks* about it can change how he *feels* about it?

# Triangles, Circles, and Arrows, Oh My!

Pick a thing or situation from your list on page 12 that makes you feel very anxious. Draw what your own triangle, circle, and arrows look like so you can better understand how your own anxiety was created.

## TRIANGLE

## CIRCLE

## ARROWS

# THREE POINTS OF ACTION

Remember that triangle we talked about? Well, that triangle is super, super important because it represents the *three points of action*. I'll explain! Even though you can make a triangle tall or short or big or small, it always has three points. That's kind of like how you and I work, too. Remember how you learned that your thoughts can change your feelings, which can change how you act? I know, it seems a little confusing, so let's break that down even more.

THOUGHTS are the things you think in your head. Most of the time, we don't think about our thoughts too much. When a bad thing happens to us, we usually think that's what causes us to have bad feelings or to take actions we might regret later. But if we look at the triangle, we can see that it's actu- ally our *thoughts* that have the most power. We can change how we feel and how we act just by changing how we *think* in a bad or scary situation.

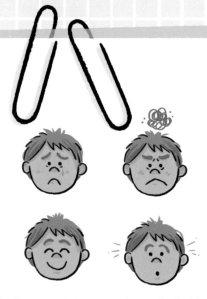

**FEELINGS** are the things you feel in your body, such as sadness, happiness, anger, jealousy, guilt, embarrassment, anxiety, and more. Sometimes we can feel one very intensely, and sometimes we feel multiple feelings at the same time. That can be very confusing. It can also feel like we're out of control of our feelings, which can make us feel, think, and act even worse. But wait! Because it is actually our thoughts that can change how we feel, not the situation we're in, we have way more control over how we feel than we first believed.

**ACTIONS** are the things you do, such as crying, yelling, running, jumping, throwing, or hiding, to name a few. We can do a lot of different actions at any given moment—some of them we actively decide in our heads to do, and sometimes it feels like our body has a mind of its own! I know I've wished that I hadn't yelled at my friend when they said something that scared me or hid under my bed when it was time to go to school. Our actions are directly linked to our thoughts and feelings, which we just learned we have more control of. Yay!

Okay, now you've got this triangle business down, does that mean you can just change the way you think by snapping your fingers? No way! It can be hard work to change the way you think, but if you take it step by step, it can feel easy breezy. Let's get started.

# YOUR NEW TOOLBOX

You've learned a lot about anxiety and now you can finally get to the best part: stopping it! You stop anxiety from bossing you around by using a special toolbox that we are going to fill with new "tools." These tools are things you can do and skills you can use when you feel your anxiety starting to boss you around, to help shrink it and make it quieter. These tools can help you at home, at school, and out in the world.

Sometimes you need different tools depending on where you are, what you're doing, who you're with, and lots of other different factors. Trying to decide which tool to use, and when, can feel overwhelming, so let's explore each area of your life so you can learn how to pick the best tools when you need them.

# Facing Scary Things

If you're scared of a bug, you should avoid that bug at all costs, right? Nope! This is a little weird but hear me out. The more you avoid the scary thing, the less time you spend with it and the scarier it becomes. That little fear of bugs becomes a big fear because you avoid them for so long that you feel too scared to even go outside. This is why it's a good idea to face things you're scared of and do as many brave activities as you can.

But if you're scared of bugs, you don't want to go out and find the biggest, grossest bug there is and plop it right on your face! The way to do it is to start out small, maybe looking at pictures of the bug, or holding a small, less threatening bug in your hand. Do you see how starting small and working your way up can help you be more successful at facing scary things?

For this activity, I want you to grab your mom or your dad (or both!) and face the *least* scary thing from your chapter 1 checklist (page 12).

Keep track of how you feel while facing your fear by filling in the table.

# My Brave Activity:

| HOW I FELT BEFORE THE BRAVE ACTIVITY | HOW I FELT DURING THE BRAVE ACTIVITY | HOW I FELT AFTER THE BRAVE ACTIVITY |
|---|---|---|
| | | |

# CHAPTER 3:

# YOU AT HOME

# HOW DO YOU FEEL WHEN YOU'RE AT HOME?

Home is a place where most of us feel safe. It's where we can go when we've had a tough day, and we almost always feel better right away. That safe feeling is great, but when you're anxious, it can be extra hard to leave that wonderful, safe feeling. If you feel bad or sad, angry or worried, and you know that home makes you feel happy and safe, it makes sense that you might not want to leave to go someplace else. Even fun places, like the movies or a friend's house, can feel unsafe when you're anxious. Staying home all the time might start to sound like a pretty good idea.

Remember learning about brave activities? This is very similar: If you never leave the good feeling that home gives you, you don't get exposed to difficult feelings you may experience outside of home. If you avoid difficult feelings, they become bigger and scarier and even more difficult. That's why it's important to treat home as your *base*, but not as a place to hide from things.

Do you remember the shapes we looked at—specifically the circle? The more you avoid bad feelings, the more anxious you get at the *thought* of feeling bad feelings; the more anxious you *feel* when you approach bad feelings, the more you *back away* from those bad feelings, and then . . . it starts over again! The circle of anxiety can make you dizzy.

So, when is it okay to want to stay home, and when should you be brave and venture out?

# GOING OUT, STAYING IN

We're going to talk more about avoiding things and how it relates to anxiety. When you think back to all the times in the past few weeks when you felt anxious, I bet a lot of them have a similar worry, like "What's going to happen?" or "What will this be like?" It's completely normal to ask yourself these questions. We all get a little nervous when we don't know what's going to happen.

Think about this: If you were going over to a friend's house for the first time, you'd probably be excited, right? You really like hanging out with this friend and can't wait to have a day full of fun activities with them. But you also feel anxious. Why is that? Because sometimes even if we're excited or happy about something, we can still get anxious about it because that something is *unknown*. We don't know what it will be like at this friend's house. Will they have food you like? Will their parents be nice? Will your friend think you're fun to spend time with? Next thing you know, you're back in that circle of worry. If you let your anxiety boss you around, maybe you would avoid going to that friend's house altogether. That is exactly what anxiety wants: It wants you to avoid unknown things, because that makes it stronger.

So, what should you do? You want to do fun things, but you don't want to feel that icky anxiety feeling that comes from facing the unknown. Let's think of dealing with the unknown like a muscle you need to exercise. When you work your arm and leg muscles by throwing balls and running around, they get bigger and stronger, right? It's the same thing with your ability to deal with the unknown! We'll call this ability the "unknown muscle." The more you don't use your unknown muscle—by avoiding unfamiliar things, for example—the weaker and smaller it gets, but the more you use it—by facing new things—the stronger and bigger it gets.

Sometimes moving from one place to another place can activate your unknown muscle. Just like it can be scary to go to a friend's house when you don't know what it will be like, it can be scary and anxiety provoking if you must move, or transition, from one place to another. You may ask yourself questions like "How long will this take?" "Who will help me if I get lost or confused?" "What if I just don't like this new place?" All those anxious thoughts can make you feel disorganized and unsure of how to start transitioning from one place to another. This is another way you can work your unknown muscle: figuring out what transitions are hardest for you and facing them.

Does this mean you have to constantly face your fears by doing brave activities and unknown muscle exercises? Whoa, whoa, whoa! That would be way too much. First, let's figure out when and how often you feel anxious, then you can better decide how to deal with it.

# How Strong Is My "Unknown Muscle"?

Answer the following questions with *True* or *False*, then check your score to see how strong your unknown muscle is.

1.  **I don't like to leave my house.**

    TRUE                FALSE

2.  **I enjoy doing new things, but sometimes I don't because I'm scared.**

    TRUE                FALSE

3.  **I don't push myself to do things that are hard because I feel worried.**

    TRUE                FALSE

4.  **I get nervous that people will think bad things about me, so I don't see my friends as much as I want to.**

    TRUE                FALSE

5.  **I feel like I need to be around my parents to be safe.**

    TRUE                FALSE

If you answered 3 or more of these questions as TRUE, it's time to get to work on strengthening your unknown muscle.

If you answered 1 to 3 of these questions as TRUE, congrats! You're already on your way to a strong unknown muscle, but there's still room for more strength.

If you answered 0 of these questions as TRUE, congrats! Your unknown muscle is strong and ready to conquer all those icky anxiety feelings you've been having.

# Making Transitions

These are the kind of transitions you make when you switch from one activity to another or leave one place and go to a different one. What follows are some transitions we all make at some point. Circle the ones you have the hardest time doing, then use the extra space at the bottom to draw or write any other transitions (not shown in this list) you struggle with.

**WAKING UP**

**GETTING READY
IN THE MORNING**

**GOING FROM HOME
TO SCHOOL**

**GOING FROM ONE SUBJECT
IN SCHOOL TO THE NEXT**

**GOING FROM RECESS
BACK TO CLASS**

**GOING FROM PLAY TIME
TO CHORE OR HOMEWORK TIME**

**BEDTIME**

**OTHER HARD TRANSITIONS:**

# WHEN DO YOU FEEL ANXIOUS AT HOME?

Okay, you've learned more about transitions and your unknown muscle; now it's time to learn about your *triggers*. Maybe you've heard your parents or your teachers say it before, or maybe you already know what I mean by "trigger." Either way, I'm going to explain what this word means when we're talking about anxiety.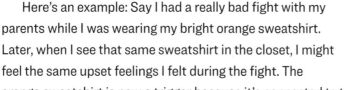

Here's an example: Say I had a really bad fight with my parents while I was wearing my bright orange sweatshirt. Later, when I see that same sweatshirt in the closet, I might feel the same upset feelings I felt during the fight. The orange sweatshirt is now a trigger because it's connected to the fight.

Here's another example: Let's say one of the things I feel anxious about is getting sick, and when my mom comes home one day coughing, I start to feel even more anxious. Later in the day I act badly toward her because her coughing triggered the anxiety I already had about getting sick.

So, anything can be a trigger, but why is this important? Well, if you know what your triggers are, you can be more prepared when you are triggered, and you can identify things you can do to help yourself and calm your anxiety.

Triggers can be small and triggers can be big. One thing can trigger lots of things, and lots of different things can trigger one thing. But don't worry! We'll figure this whole thing out. The best way to start is by learning how you can better explain your anxiety. The first step is to figure out your level of anxiety with different triggers. Some triggers will cause big and loud anxiety, while other triggers will cause small and quiet anxiety. The next few exercises are going to help you identify your triggers and level of anxiety.

# Triggers

This activity is broken into two parts. In the first part, you'll identify as many of your triggers as you can from memory. In the second part, you're going to track your triggers as they happen throughout a week, which will make you feel confident that you understand how your triggers work.

## PART I

Fill in the blanks to help you learn about some of your triggers.

**Whenever** _____ **happens,**
(situation or event)

**I feel** _____ **, which can then lead to**
(emotion)

_____ .
(a behavior and/or second emotion)

**Whenever** _____ **happens,**
(situation or event)

**I feel** _____ **, which can then lead to**
(emotion)

_____ .
(a behavior and/or second emotion)

**Whenever** _____ **happens,**
(situation or event)

**I feel** _____ **, which can then lead to**
(emotion)

_____ .
(a behavior and/or second emotion)

# PART II

For this part of the triggers exercise, you're going to keep track of what situations and events trigger specific emotions (feelings) or behaviors. Each day of the week on the chart has its own section for triggers, emotions, and behaviors. So, on Monday you'll write down what triggers you notice that day in the column titled "Trigger." On that same day you will write down what emotion came from the trigger and then what behavior resulted from that emotion. You'll do this every day of the week.

|  | TRIGGER | EMOTION | BEHAVIOR |
|---|---|---|---|
| Monday |  |  |  |
| Tuesday |  |  |  |
| Wednesday |  |  |  |
| Thursday |  |  |  |
| Friday |  |  |  |
| Saturday |  |  |  |
| Sunday |  |  |  |

# How Much Is a Lot?

Now let's figure out how big or small your anxiety can be, by numbering it. The higher the number, the bigger the anxiety. The lower the number, the smaller the anxiety. In the first column are the numbers from biggest down to smallest. In the second column, write down situations, behaviors, or triggers connected to that level of anxiety. So, your biggest trigger would be in the 10 row, while something that makes you only a little bit anxious would be in the 1 row.

| | |
|---|---|
| 10 | |
| 9 | |
| 8 | |
| 7 | |
| 6 | |
| 5 | |
| 4 | |
| 3 | |
| 2 | |
| 1 | |

# WHAT IS YOUR ANXIETY TELLING YOU?

 Anxiety has a lot it wants to tell us. Sometimes it can feel like anxiety is in complete control because it's so busy telling us to avoid certain places or people, or telling us to act in ways we wouldn't normally act. Remember when I told you that it is not actually the situation that causes anxiety, but your *thoughts* about the situation? Let's think back to the triangle—how thoughts, feelings, and actions all interact—and take a look at a situation Fatima found herself in.

Fatima lost her favorite stuffed animal, Mr. Teddy. She hasn't seen him for three whole days. She usually takes him with her everywhere. She feels very worried and sad that she'll never see him again. She also feels anxious that her mother will think she's not responsible with her toys.

What is making Fatima anxious? Many people would say it was losing Mr. Teddy, but it is really her *thoughts* about losing Mr. Teddy that trigger her anxiety. If Fatima thinks "I lost Mr. Teddy, and losing him means my mom won't think I'm a responsible person," then of course she would feel very anxious and sad. But what if Fatima thinks "I lost Mr. Teddy, but maybe I can find him. If I can't find him, I need to figure out the best way to make sure this doesn't happen again"? If Fatima has these friendlier kinds of thoughts, she probably won't feel so anxious. She may still feel a little sad or a little concerned, but not as bad as she feels when her anxious thoughts are bossing her around.

So, what can you do to turn bossy, anxious thoughts into friendlier ones?

You can make a STOP plan. S.T.O.P. stands for

**S**ituations and triggers

**T**houghts and feelings

**O**ther ways to think

**P**lan of action for change

The STOP plan can help you challenge your anxious thoughts instead of automatically doing what they tell you. Then, you find new ways to think and act that make you feel less anxious and more in control.

**S:** Figure out exactly what **situation** you are in and what **triggers** caused your bad feeling.

**T:** Identify all the bad **thoughts** you're having about the situation, about others, or about yourself, and all the different **feelings** you have along with those thoughts.

**O:** This is the most important section because this is where you figure out **other ways to think**. In other words, how to change the bad thoughts into different thoughts.

**P:** This is the **planning** part, where you figure out what behaviors or actions you're using that help cause your bad feelings, and which new positive coping tools you can use to help you start changing them.

Let's learn a little bit more about the behavior part and then you'll get the chance to practice your own STOP plan.

# Hypothesis Testing

*Hypothesis* is a pretty big word you may not have heard before. What does it mean? A hypothesis is a suggested explanation for why something is happening or how it works. When you test a hypothesis, you're trying to figure out if the explanation is true.

Hypothesis testing is an experiment to find out if an explanation that we believe is actually correct. For example: I believe that if I use my belly breathing, I will feel calmer. To test if this is correct, I would need to use my belly breathing whenever I wasn't feeling calm.

Let's break hypothesis testing down step by step:

1.  **Ask a question.**

2.  **Find out as much information about the question as you can.**

3.  **Identify your hypothesis (your guess at the answer to the question).**

4.  **Test the hypothesis.**

5.  **Look at the results of the experiment and come up with your answer (was your question right or wrong?).**

Here's an example of how to use hypothesis testing when you're feeling anxious about something.

1.  **Question:** Will my friends stop liking me if I get a bad grade?

2.  **Information:**

    My friends have never said they wouldn't like me if I got a bad grade.
    My friends have probably gotten bad grades, too.
    My friends are usually nice.
    I'll feel bad about myself if I get a bad grade.

3.  **Hypothesis:** My friends will probably like me even if I get a bad grade.

4.  **Test:** When I get a bad grade, tell my friends.

5.  **Results:** My friends supported me and told me of course they still like me.

## Hypothesis Testing, *continued*

Can you see how hypothesis testing can help you figure out what question you want to ask and how to challenge it? There are many different ways you can use hypothesis testing to stop your anxiety from bossing you around. Why don't you give hypothesis testing a whirl?

1.  **Question:** _____

    _____

    _____

2.  **Information:** _____

    _____

    _____

3.  **Hypothesis:** _____

    _____

    _____

4.  **Test:** _____

    _____

    _____

5.  **Results:** _____

    _____

    _____

# Possible Versus Probable

Now let's learn the difference between *possible* and *probable*. The words sound pretty similar, and in some ways they are, but there's also a very important difference between them.

**Possible:** Something that is *able* to be done, or something that *may* happen. For example, I could *possibly* walk 10 miles to a store, because I am physically able to do that.

**Probable:** Something that is *likely* to be done, or to happen. Something that has a better chance of happening than not happening. I could *possibly* walk 10 miles to the store, but it's not very likely. It's more *probable* that Mom or Dad will drive me in our car.

These two words are important because anxiety *loves* to make you think that *possible* things are actually *probable*, when that is not the case! It's good to practice identifying situations that are possible or probable so you can keep up your best effort in showing anxiety who's the boss.

Read the situations on the left and make a check mark under **Possible**, **Probable**, or **Not Likely**:

| | POSSIBLE | PROBABLE | NOT LIKELY |
|---|---|---|---|
| Your friends will be mad at you for getting a bad grade. | | | |
| You will catch a sickness just from thinking about it. | | | |
| You ask your parents for help. | | | |
| You make a mistake. | | | |
| You will get a stomachache from everything you eat. | | | |
| Someone will judge you. | | | |

# STOP Plan: At Home

You've got a lot of tools in your toolbox, and you've learned lots of great ways to help fight your anxiety. Now that you know about hypothesis testing and all about the STOP plan, let's practice making a STOP plan just for you.

First, let's practice with an example.

**Situations and triggers:** I'm invited to a birthday party where I won't know anyone.

**Thoughts and feelings:** I *feel* scared, anxious, and excited. I *think* there is a chance no one will like me. I also *think* I'm not fun enough to go to a birthday party.

**Other ways to think:** There is no *probable* reason the other kids won't like me. I won't know if I'll get along with the other kids unless I actually go to the party. I can use this as a *brave activity*. My mom tells me that I am fun.

**Plan of action toward change:** I'll go to the birthday party and use some of my coping tools to help keep me calm. I'll also ask my mom to support me.

Now, fill out your plan!

| S | |
|---|---|
| T | |
| O | |
| P | |

# LET'S TRY SOMETHING NEW

So far, we've talked about *feelings* and we've talked about *thoughts*—but there's still one point left on the triangle. What role does your *behavior*—how you act—play? You've learned that your thoughts, emotions, and behaviors can all influence one another. Now let's really focus on your behaviors to understand how the way you behave can affect how anxious you feel.

But first, I want to talk about choice. A lot of times, it might seem like you don't choose how you feel or behave or what you think. This is especially true when you're anxious and upset—when you think or do certain things, it feels like you can't help it. But I have good news: You can *always* choose how you act. In fact, you have much more control over your thoughts and actions than you think. Let's look at an example.

José is anxious about his upcoming birthday. He thinks about it all the time. He's worried no one will come to the party if he plans one, and he worries his mom and dad will forget it's his birthday and he won't get any presents. His mom tells him he has nothing to worry about, but José doesn't believe her. He tells his mom he doesn't want a party. Then, he goes to some other kids' birthday parties and sees how much fun they are, whether there are five people or fifty people there. José realizes he can't know ahead of time how many people will come to his party, but he decides to face his fear and let his mom send out the invitations. The day of the party he feels very nervous, but as people start to show up, he doesn't even think to count the guests because he is having too much fun!

Can you see how José *decided* to behave in a different way? He didn't try to avoid what he felt anxious about by canceling his party. And afterward, he felt a lot better. Like José, you always have the power to choose how you behave. Even when you don't have much control over what is going on, you always have control over what you do. That can be a very powerful thing to realize.

Sometimes it can be difficult to remember you have that choice. The tougher the situation, the harder it is to remember you have a choice, which means you need a plan for remembering your ability to choose. Let's figure out different, or *alternative*, behaviors that you can use instead of the ones that keep you feeling anxious. These alternative behaviors will be difficult to do at first, because you're not used to doing them. Use the next few activities to build your STOP plan.

# Alternative Behaviors

You know what an alternative behavior is (something you can do instead), but you may not know which behaviors are negative, and how to replace them with positive ones. Here are some negative behaviors that usually help anxiety stick around.

1. **Avoidance**
2. **Throwing things**
3. **Yelling**
4. **Fighting**
5. **Ignoring**

Think of a few negative behaviors you may do at home and write them down.

1. _____
2. _____
3. _____
4. _____
5. _____

Now let's look at some positive behaviors.

1. **Talking it out**
2. **Taking some deep breaths**
3. **Facing our fears/doing brave activities**
4. **Asking for help**
5. **Using a coping skill**

Think of a few positive behaviors you can do at home and write them on the lines.

1. _____
2. _____
3. _____
4. _____
5. _____

# Rating Our Behaviors

Before you can make a plan for using your positive alternative behaviors, you need to set yourself up to succeed by planning for possible setbacks. One of the ways you can do this is by rating your new positive behaviors. Why rate them? Because planning to use a really difficult alternative behavior in a really difficult situation would not be setting yourself up to succeed. It's better to plan to use easier alternative behaviors in tougher situations, so you don't feel overwhelmed.

In the table, write the alternative positive behaviors you already defined in the Easy, Medium, or Hard columns. For example, if you find it pretty easy to talk with your mom, write "talking it out" in the Easy column. If doing brave activities feels really hard, put that in the Hard column.

| EASY ALTERNATIVE BEHAVIORS | MEDIUM ALTERNATIVE BEHAVIORS | HARD ALTERNATIVE BEHAVIORS |
| --- | --- | --- |
|  |  |  |
|  |  |  |
|  |  |  |
|  |  |  |
|  |  |  |
|  |  |  |

# Making a Plan

Now, you can make a plan so you know exactly what to do when you notice you're falling into negative behavior patterns. This activity is just like the trigger activity, except instead of just identifying triggers, you're also going to identify an alternative, positive behavior you can use.

Whenever _____ happens,
(situation or event)

I feel _____, which can then lead to
(emotion)

_____. I plan to stop this negative
(a negative behavior)

behavior by replacing it with _____.
(a positive behavior)

Whenever _____ happens,
(situation or event)

I feel _____, which can then lead to
(emotion)

_____. I plan to stop this negative
(a negative behavior)

behavior by replacing it with _____.
(a positive behavior)

Whenever _____ happens,
(situation or event)

I feel _____, which can then lead to
(emotion)

_____. I plan to stop this negative
(a negative behavior)

behavior by replacing it with _____.
(a positive behavior)

# Facing the Things That Scare You at Home

We've talked about the importance of facing the things that scare you and doing brave activities. Remember the example of the bug? How if you're super scared of a bug you actually need to face that bug in order to overcome your fear? You picked one scary thing to face and came up with a brave activity to complete, and even though it must have been very difficult to do, you did it! It feels great to accomplish something, even if it's a hard process.

Sometimes we need to learn how to *accept* difficult things, instead of avoiding or worrying about them. Acceptance can be super hard. Luckily, there are lots of different strategies you can use to help yourself accept difficult things. These strategies are important because they're going to help you overcome the negative thoughts and feelings you have.

When you worry, obsess, or avoid things, it usually keeps you stuck in one place. Accepting things can help you move forward. But how can you learn to be more accepting? Here are some different ways to do that.

- **Let your feelings happen.** When you feel a certain feeling, like anxiety, let it come! Be "mindful," or aware of the feeling. Breathe through the feeling. Don't feel that you have to change the feeling or stop it from coming. Sometimes we need to feel bad before we can start to feel better. You don't need to judge yourself based on a feeling you are having, and remember—no feeling lasts forever.

- **Focus on your strengths.** Instead of thinking about all the ways you think you could be better or do better, focus on what you're good at.

- **Allow yourself to have weaknesses.** Just like you should focus on your strengths, you should allow yourself to have weaknesses. Everyone has weaknesses. Sometimes it is our weaknesses that make us stronger, happier, and whole!

- **Don't try to be perfect.** You've heard it before: *No one* is perfect. It's still true; it's impossible to be perfect. Life is about learning, and you can't learn unless you make some mistakes.

- **Allow difficult things to happen without trying to avoid or escape them.** At some point you'll lose something you love, get in a fight with your parent, feel anxious, or make a mistake and have to deal with the consequences. Instead of constantly trying to prevent, avoid, or escape it, learn how to accept it. When you focus on what you *can* control instead of the things you *can't* control, you start to really show anxiety who's the boss.

- **Understand that you are always in control of how you think, even if you don't have control over a specific situation.** Remember, it is not the situation that causes you to feel a certain way, it is your thoughts, so even if you have no control over a situation, you still always have control over yourself.

Now that you've armed yourself with these acceptance skills, grab a grown-up helper and get started.

**Step 1:** Identify what you're scared of.

**Step 2:** Figure out when you're going to do your brave activity.

**Step 3:** Identify how to calm down when the scary thing becomes too scary.

Use the next few pages to write your very own brave activity plan.

# Brave Activity Plan

Make sure you have your grown-up helper with you while you're creating and doing your brave activity plan. Start with the least scary thing (1) and work your way up to the scariest thing (10).

| | FEAR<br>What scares you? | BRAVE ACTIVITY<br>How are you going to face your fear? | WHEN<br>When do you plan to do your brave activity? | COPING<br>What skills can you use to help calm yourself down? |
|---|---|---|---|---|
| 1 | | | | |
| 2 | | | | |
| 3 | | | | |
| 4 | | | | |
| 5 | | | | |

|  | FEAR | BRAVE ACTIVITY | WHEN | COPING |
|---|---|---|---|---|
| 6 |  |  |  |  |
| 7 |  |  |  |  |
| 8 |  |  |  |  |
| 9 |  |  |  |  |
| 10 |  |  |  |  |

# CHAPTER 4

# YOU AT SCHOOL

# HOW DO YOU FEEL AT SCHOOL?

School is a fun place to learn and grow. At school, you get to see your friends, try new things, and learn all sorts of cool stuff. But new experiences can also bring new worries—sometimes a lot of them. Whether it is something new, something you experience every day, or a future worry, there are many different points in the day where anxiety can start bossing you around and make you begin to feel like school is the problem. As you've already learned, you have way more control than you think you do. School isn't the problem; it's that sneaky anxiety that's controlling you and making you feel bad about a place that can be super fun.

There are many reasons you could feel anxious at school; one might be the social part—your friends, classmates, teachers, and all sorts of other people. Let's hear about José.

José is in the second grade, and every day he begs his mother to stay home from school. He doesn't want to go to school because he worries he has no friends. Every day at recess he asks to go to the bathroom or to the nurse, and he begins to cry if the teacher announces a group project. He is anxious that if the other kids find out he doesn't have any friends, they will bully him.

He's worried that there's something wrong with him, and that's why no one ever asks him to play.

Poor José! He keeps avoiding recess and group projects instead of facing his fear. José is also behaving in a way that makes it difficult for other kids to ask him to join in because he is never at recess or available when picking partners for group projects.

Maybe if José learned some coping strategies, asked for help, and did some brave activities, or thought about his own strengths, he would feel a lot better. After everything you've learned so far, what would you tell José to do to start showing anxiety who's boss?

# Kids Like ME!

Here are some more stories that will help you understand that most kids feel worried or scared about *something* at school. It will also help you get better at figuring out what your own worries may be.

## LIZZY

Lizzy is in the fifth grade and she worries a lot about tests. She studies for hours and hours but still worries that she doesn't know the right information. Sometimes, when she is taking a test, she will freeze and not be able to remember stuff she knew perfectly the night before. What are some of the thoughts Lizzy may be having?

-----------------------------------------------

-----------------------------------------------

-----------------------------------------------

## NOAH

Noah is in the third grade and he fears eating or using the bathroom at school. He worries that if he eats something that upsets his stomach, he will get sick at school. He also worries that someone may hear him use the bathroom and think bad things about him. Noah tries to hold it for the whole school day! He avoids drinking water or eating food for the whole day, too. How could avoiding eating or using the bathroom make Noah's anxiety even worse? What thoughts do you think he is having?

-----------------------------------------------

-----------------------------------------------

-----------------------------------------------

# JAMAL

Jamal is in the second grade and is scared to be away from his parents. He worries that something bad may happen to them if he is not with them every second of every day. Every morning he tells them he is sick, and he tries whatever he can to avoid school and stay with them. Can you guess why Jamal's behavior is making him feel even more anxious?

------------------------------------------------------------

------------------------------------------------------------

------------------------------------------------------------

# School-Time Feelings

School can come with a lot of different feelings, and it can be confusing to figure out exactly how you feel. Maybe you know you feel "bad," but you can't really explain how. Well, you know that your feelings can affect your thoughts, which can also affect your behavior. Here is a list of feelings that most of us have. Think about the last time you felt each feeling at school and describe it in the space below the words.

**Mad**

---------------------------------------------------------

---------------------------------------------------------

---------------------------------------------------------

**Sad**

---------------------------------------------------------

---------------------------------------------------------

---------------------------------------------------------

**Jealous**

---------------------------------------------------------

---------------------------------------------------------

---------------------------------------------------------

### School-Time Feelings, *continued*

**Scared**

------------------------------------------------

------------------------------------------------

------------------------------------------------

**Embarrassed**

------------------------------------------------

------------------------------------------------

------------------------------------------------

**Proud**

------------------------------------------------

------------------------------------------------

------------------------------------------------

# WHEN DO YOU FEEL ANXIOUS AT SCHOOL?

School is a place you see your friends, but it's also a place where you are tested and graded. It's a place where teachers watch what you do, then tell you whether you're doing it right. This happens when you take tests and do homework. There's also the chance that a teacher might call on you in class to answer a question. You may worry that you'll give the wrong answer or say the wrong word, and so your heart starts to beat a mile a minute and you can't even focus on what the teacher is saying. That would make school a really tough place to be, wouldn't it?

Not knowing what makes you worried is kind of like going into a dark room without a flashlight. You can put your hands out to help you figure out where to walk, but a flashlight would help you see exactly where to go. Going to school and feeling anxious without knowing what is causing your anxiety is like walking around in the dark. It will likely make you feel even *more* anxious! It also makes you more likely to think school is a place you should avoid.

Remember when we talked about triggers? Triggers can be complicated. You learned that you can have small triggers and large triggers. One thing can trigger multiple things and multiple things can trigger one thing. It all seemed confusing at first, but you figured it out. Now you can apply your knowledge to school, too.

Your anxiety about school may be triggered by leaving the safety of your home, or the safety of your parents. Or a fear of being laughed at may be a trigger for you. School is a crowded place; maybe that feels overwhelming. Some of your fears may be related to social fears, others related to how you do in your schoolwork, and some may be related to something very specific, like seeing a spider on the playground.

**Social** fears are ones that involve the other kids at school. Being scared to speak in front of your classmates, not getting picked for team sports, or being made fun of are all *social* worries. Other kids can be unpredictable, and that can be scary. You can never know for sure why other kids act the way they do. For example, another kid could say something mean to you because they feel bad about themselves, or maybe they do something bad because they feel scared and sad. A kid could yell because they're used to lots of yelling at home, or they may stop talking completely and freeze because they're nervous about what other kids may think of them.

**Performance** fears have to do with tests, homework, and grades. School is all about learning, and the main way teachers figure out how well you understand your work is by giving you grades. Grades are good for some things, but they can make kids feel very worried. Nobody ever wants to get a bad grade, but it's also not possible to be perfect.

**Specific** fears are what we call "phobias." Usually, when someone has a phobia, they do anything they can to avoid what scares them. If you had a specific fear that you had to face at school, then school would become a very scary place! Here are some common specific fears, or phobias:

HEIGHTS          SPIDERS          NEEDLES          GERMS          CROWDS

Now that you know more about what anxiety can be like at school, you can be on the lookout for the ways school anxiety might try to boss you around. The next few activities will help you figure out what triggers your own anxieties, so you can shine a flashlight on them and not be wandering around in the dark!

# School-Time Scaries!

In the chart is a list of common school-time worries. Put a check mark under the column that shows how often you feel worried about that specific situation: Never, Sometimes, or Often. Afterward, look at how you filled in the table. Can you tell what kinds of things scare you most?

| SITUATION | NEVER | SOMETIMES | OFTEN |
|---|---|---|---|
| Being away from my parents | | | |
| Being laughed at | | | |
| Getting a bad grade | | | |
| Feeling crowded | | | |
| Feeling scared to be around someone who is sick or being around all the germs | | | |
| Worrying about what will happen at lunch or recess | | | |
| Playing sports during gym/PE | | | |
| Saying something wrong | | | |
| Being called on in class | | | |
| Getting sick at school | | | |
| Using the bathroom at school | | | |

# My Flashlight

Take a look at the two flashlights. One is a little smaller than the other. That's because one flashlight is for the worries you put in the Sometimes column and the other is for the worries you put in the Often column. Fill in the beams with all your school worries so you'll be prepared for any dark day.

# WHAT IS YOUR ANXIETY TELLING YOU?

As you've learned, anxiety has *a lot* it wants to tell you. Remember you learned that it can feel like anxiety is in control of you because it starts telling you where to go and how to act? This is still very true for you at school. You know there are lots of ways your anxiety can be triggered. Let's see what a school trigger may look like.

Yuki feels very nervous about how his classmates see him. He is scared they think he is not smart. One morning as he is rushing to get ready, his mother tells him he really needs to hurry up so he isn't late. This triggers Yuki to panic and he becomes *very* anxious because he doesn't want to walk into the classroom late and have all his classmates stare at him.

Yuki's trigger is his mom telling him to hurry, but he may have all sorts of different triggers. If he already knew about his triggers, he would have a better chance of dealing with them when they happen.

Let's look at a different example so you can learn more about how your thoughts about school anxiety can change how you feel.

Emma is in the fourth grade. She loves science and art. Her friends think she is funny and smart. One day, Emma gets a bad grade on a test and starts to feel very anxious.

What is making Emma anxious? Many people would say it was the bad grade, but really it is her *thoughts* about the bad grade that make her anxious. If Emma thinks "I got a bad grade and a bad grade must mean I'm not smart. My friends won't like me if I'm not smart, and my family will be very disappointed in me if I don't always do well," then *of course* she would feel very anxious.

But what if Emma thinks "I got a bad grade on this test, but it's only one test. I feel sad about getting a bad grade, but I'll try harder next time," or if she thinks "Everyone gets a bad grade at some point, so why would my family or friends think badly of me when I tried my best?" If Emma has these thoughts, it is likely that she will not feel anxious. She may feel a little sad, a little concerned, but definitely not anxious. Can you see how the *situation* is still the same? Emma still got a bad grade, but her *feeling* is different because of the way she thinks about the situation.

On the next few pages you'll do some more hypothesis testing, learn more about probable and possible situations at school, and create a STOP plan for school anxieties.

# Hypothesis Testing

Let's put hypothesis testing to work, but this time we'll focus on school-related anxieties. First, here's a refresher on the step-by-step process of hypothesis testing:

1.   **Ask a question.**

2.   **Find out as much information about the question as you can.**

3.   **Identify your hypothesis (your guess at the answer to the question).**

4.   **Test the hypothesis.**

5.   **Look at the results of the experiment and come up with your answer (was your question right or wrong?).**

Okay, let's get started!

1.   **Question:** _____

     _____

     _____

2.   **Information:** _____

     _____

     _____

3. **Hypothesis:** _____

_____

_____

4. **Test:** _____

_____

_____

5. **Results:** _____

_____

_____

# Possible Versus Probable

You're an expert at figuring out if a situation is possible or probable at home—but what about in school? Let's identify some worries you have at school and categorize them as *possible* or *probable*. First, here's a refresher on the definition of possible and probable:

**Possible:** Something that is *able* to be done. Something that *may* happen.

**Probable:** Something that is *likely* to happen. Something that has a better chance of happening than not happening.

Now come up with your list of school-time worries:

1. _____

2. _____

3. _____

4. _____

5. _____

Write your worries in the proper category: Possible or Probable.

| POSSIBLE | PROBABLE |
|---|---|
|  |  |
|  |  |
|  |  |
|  |  |
|  |  |

# STOP Plan: At School

This time you'll fill out your STOP plan with something that has to do with school. It can be about performance, related to social situations, or be something specific. Here's a refresher on the STOP plan:

SITUATIONS AND TRIGGERS

THOUGHTS AND FEELINGS

OTHER WAYS TO THINK

PLAN OF ACTION TOWARD CHANGE

Now, fill out your very own school STOP plan.

| | |
|---|---|
| **S** | |
| **T** | |
| **O** | |
| **P** | |

# LET'S TRY SOMETHING NEW

You've learned about choice and how a lot of times it doesn't seem like you choose how you feel, behave, or think—that it just happens. But you know that's not the case and that you do have control over these things. Let's read about how Sarah's behaviors at school affected how she felt.

Sarah is anxious about germs. She worries that she will get a cold because many of the other kids in her classroom have gotten sick. She begins to think about it all the time and begs her mother to let her stay home from school, but her mother makes her go. Sarah avoids her friends, just in case they're sick. But she starts to feel lonely and realizes that she doesn't feel any better after avoiding her fear all morning. She chooses to face her fear and play with a friend at recess. So she chooses to use some of her coping strategies to keep calm while she is playing, and although she feels very anxious at first, she begins to feel a lot calmer and she even has some fun.

Can you see how Sarah *decided* to behave in a different way? In other words, she chose to not avoid what she was anxious about, and she felt a lot better afterward. Remember, you *always* have a choice in how you behave or act in any situation. Even if you don't have much control over what is going on, you always have control over what you do.

You already know what alternative behaviors are, so now let's figure out your school-time plan for behaving differently. Just like your home alternative behaviors, they'll be difficult to do at first because you're not used to doing them. On the next few pages, you're going to figure out your negative behaviors at school and what positive behaviors you can replace them with. Then you're going to make a behavior plan for school.

# Alternative Behaviors

You know what an alternative behavior is, but you may not know which behaviors are negative and how to replace them with positive ones. First, let's define some negative behaviors that usually help anxiety stick around.

1.  **Avoidance (avoiding recess, lunch, etc.)**
2.  **Ignoring friends**
3.  **Yelling**
4.  **Fighting**
5.  **Refusing to do your schoolwork**

Think of a few negative behaviors you may do at school and write them on the lines.

1. _____

2. _____

3. _____

4. _____

5. _____

Now let's define some positive behaviors.

1.  **Talking it out with a teacher or a friend**
2.  **Taking some deep breaths**
3.  **Facing your fears/doing brave activities**
4.  **Asking for help**
5.  **Using a coping skill**

Think of a few positive behaviors you can do at school and write them down.

1. _____

2. _____

3. _____

4. _____

5. _____

# Rating Our Behaviors

Remember, before you can make a plan for using your positive alternative behaviors, you need to set yourself up to succeed. In the table, write down the alternative behaviors you defined and assign them to the Easy, Medium, or Hard columns.

| EASY ALTERNATIVE BEHAVIORS | MEDIUM ALTERNATIVE BEHAVIORS | HARD ALTERNATIVE BEHAVIORS |
|---|---|---|
| | | |
| | | |
| | | |
| | | |
| | | |
| | | |

# Making a Plan

Now, you can make a plan so you know exactly what to do when you notice you're falling into negative behavior patterns. This activity is like the trigger activity in the last chapter, except instead of just identifying triggers, you're also going to identify an alternative positive behavior you can use.

Whenever _____ happens,
**(situation or event)**

I feel _____, which can then lead to
**(emotion)**

_____. I plan to stop this negative
**(a negative behavior)**

behavior by replacing it with _____.
**(a positive behavior)**

Whenever _____ happens,
**(situation or event)**

I feel _____, which can then lead to
**(emotion)**

_____. I plan to stop this negative
**(a negative behavior)**

behavior by replacing it with _____.
**(a positive behavior)**

Whenever _____ happens,
**(situation or event)**

I feel _____, which can then lead to
**(emotion)**

_____. I plan to stop this negative
**(a negative behavior)**

behavior by replacing it with _____.
**(a positive behavior)**

# Facing the Things That Scare You at School

You know what comes next: brave activities! But first, here are the acceptance strategies you learned in the last chapter, but this time focused on accepting scary or uncomfortable things at school.

- **Let your feelings happen.** It's okay to feel sad if you get a bad grade. Letting yourself feel sad is part of the learning process and is necessary in order to feel better. If you feel angry at someone for ignoring you at lunch or for being picked last at recess, that's okay. If you accept your feelings without being hard on yourself, it's much easier to move forward from them.

- **Focus on your strengths.** If you got a bad grade in math, remember that you aced your reading assignment. If you're struggling with school assignments, remember that you're a good friend. There are always both negatives and positives, and recognizing those positives can be very helpful in fighting anxiety.

- **Allow yourself to make mistakes.** You've already learned that *everyone* makes mistakes. This is especially important to remember at school, where performance is a big part of the day. Remember that mistakes are what make us stronger!

- **Don't try to be perfect.** It may sound corny, but it's true: No one is perfect. You may think the other kids don't have any problems, or that everyone else understands the math problem except you, but that's your anxiety trying to boss you around. It's not the truth! It's so important to recognize when your expectations for yourself are too high, because that just sets you up to fail. *No one* is perfect, and *everyone* has their own struggles, even if they seem to have it totally together. Some of them may even have anxiety, just like you.

- **Allow hard things to happen without trying to avoid them.** At some point, you'll get a bad grade. Or you'll get picked last for kickball. Or you'll say the wrong answer when your teacher calls on you. I know, it's awful to hear that, but it's important to accept it. At some point you'll get into a fight with your best friend. At some point you'll say something that embarrasses you. Do you see where this is going? It's impossible to avoid bad or difficult things, and that is no different at school. Remember what you learned: Focus on what you *can* control and not on what you can't control.

- **Understand that you can choose how you think about the situation you're in—even if you can't choose the situation.** You may have tried your hardest on that last test, and now that it's over you can't control anything else about it. But you *can* choose what kind of thoughts you have about it, which will affect how you feel and behave. You have more power than you think!

Now, just like last time, grab a grown-up helper and get to work. Here's a reminder on your steps:

**Step 1:** Identify what you're scared of at school.

**Step 2:** Figure out when you're going to do your brave activity.

**Step 3:** Identify how to calm down when the scary thing becomes too scary.

Alright, it's time to make your own brave activity plan.

# Brave Activity Plan

Make sure you have your grown-up helper with you while you're creating and doing your brave activity plan. Start with the least scary thing (1) and work your way up to the scariest thing (10).

| | FEAR<br>What scares you? | BRAVE ACTIVITY<br>How are you going to face your fear? | WHEN<br>When do you plan to do your brave activity? | COPING<br>What skills can you use to help calm yourself down? |
|---|---|---|---|---|
| 1 | | | | |
| 2 | | | | |
| 3 | | | | |
| 4 | | | | |
| 5 | | | | |

|  | FEAR | BRAVE ACTIVITY | WHEN | COPING |
|---|---|---|---|---|
| 6 | | | | |
| 7 | | | | |
| 8 | | | | |
| 9 | | | | |
| 10 | | | | |

# CHAPTER 5:

# YOU IN THE WORLD

# HOW DO YOU FEEL WHEN YOU'RE OUT?

Now you know all about your anxiety when you're at home and school. Next, we're going to focus on what anxieties may come up when you're out and about. Remember you learned about how transitions can be scary? Well, they can be especially scary or anxiety provoking when you're transitioning from one place to another. The fear could be even

bigger if you're transitioning to a place you've never been before. Let's read about Ayla.

Ayla is a nine-year-old girl with a very busy Saturday coming up. First, she has to go to her brother's basketball game, then she is going with her family and some of her brother's friends to a restaurant she has never been to. Ayla wonders what her brother's friends will be like—sometimes in the past they've teased her or been really mean. She also wonders what the restaurant will be like—what if she gets a stomachache and is far away from home? What if she doesn't like any of the food but can't go home for hours and so is very hungry? After the restaurant, Ayla is going to see a movie with her friend Sari and Sari's parents. Ayla wonders if the movie will be scary. She is afraid she'll get scared and Sari won't want to be her friend anymore. What if she feels sick from the restaurant and doesn't even want to go to the movies? Will Sari be mad at her?

Look at all of Ayla's anxious thoughts! It's no wonder she feels out of control whenever she goes out into the world. It also wouldn't be very surprising if Ayla

does not have a very fun day, which is silly because she's going to do things she loves: going out to eat, spending time with her family, and watching a movie with her friend. If Ayla let anxiety boss her around, maybe she would beg her mom to stay home or fake a sickness so she could avoid all of it. Then she would miss out on the things she loves. The more Ayla tries to stay home and avoid the things that worry her, the louder and more in control her anxiety gets. It's just like that bouncy ball we talked about back in chapter 1.

Transitions aren't the only thing kids like you worry about. There are a ton of other things that can be triggers for anxiety. Your first step is to figure out your own triggers when you're out in the world. Then you can start to do something about it.

# Places Where I Feel Anxious

The following are a bunch of different situations or things that may trigger someone out in the world. Circle the ones that you feel apply to you. In the second section, write down some other situations, things, or transitions not listed in the first section so you can get a better idea of your unique triggers.

A NEW RESTAURANT

A FRIEND'S HOUSE

A CROWDED PLACE

AN UNFAMILIAR PLACE

ON A PLANE

GOING TO SEVERAL DIFFERENT PLACES WITHOUT GOING HOME FIRST

I feel anxious when I . . .

- - - - - - - - - - - - - - - - - - - - - - - - - - - - - - - - - - - - - -  - - - - - - - - - - - - - - - - - - - - - - - - - - - - - - - - - - - - - -

- - - - - - - - - - - - - - - - - - - - - - - - - - - - - - - - - - - - - -  - - - - - - - - - - - - - - - - - - - - - - - - - - - - - - - - - - - - - -

- - - - - - - - - - - - - - - - - - - - - - - - - - - - - - - - - - - - - -  - - - - - - - - - - - - - - - - - - - - - - - - - - - - - - - - - - - - - -

- - - - - - - - - - - - - - - - - - - - - - - - - - - - - - - - - - - - - -  - - - - - - - - - - - - - - - - - - - - - - - - - - - - - - - - - - - - - -

- - - - - - - - - - - - - - - - - - - - - - - - - - - - - - - - - - - - - -  - - - - - - - - - - - - - - - - - - - - - - - - - - - - - - - - - - - - - -

# How Much Is a Lot?

Now let's number how big or small your anxiety can be. You've done something like this before, but this time you're going to number all the situations you identified in the last activity. Remember, the higher the number, the bigger the anxiety. The lower the number, the smaller the anxiety. In the first column is the number from biggest down to smallest. The second column is where you'll write down situations, behaviors, or triggers connected to that level of anxiety.

| | |
|---|---|
| 10 | |
| 9 | |
| 8 | |
| 7 | |
| 6 | |
| 5 | |
| 4 | |
| 3 | |
| 2 | |
| 1 | |

# PEOPLE, PLACES & THINGS

Sometimes a place is scary one day and then the next it doesn't feel as scary. Or maybe it's not a place that makes you feel anxious; maybe it's a specific person or even a specific thing. The first step in showing anxiety who's boss is to discover your triggers, right? Let's hear stories about a few kids and see what they discovered their triggers to be.

Anya knows exactly what her trigger is: dogs. She is terrified of all of them. She won't go to a friend's house if they have a dog. Once she almost ran out into the street to try to get away from a dog. That was very scary for Anya and her parents. She usually feels her heart start to race when she even thinks of a dog and sometimes gets very sweaty. Anya is ready to work on her anxiety, just like you've decided to work on yours.

Anya's anxiety is what we call a specific phobia, which is another type of anxiety. A specific phobia is not just related to dogs; it can be an intense fear about anything, such as bugs, snakes, elevators, planes, and much, much more. Everyone is scared of something, but a specific phobia makes you avoid your fear at any cost.

Greyson is not always scared of movie theaters. He is only scared when they are full of people. The problem is that Greyson never knows if the movie theater will be crowded or not. His mother has tried to convince him that everything is safe, but he feels very uncomfortable and sick

83

whenever he walks into the dark theater and sees all those people in the seats. His mother once took him to an early morning show so he could feel sure it wouldn't be crowded. Even though there were only a few people there, he couldn't stop wondering if more people were going to come in. He couldn't watch the movie and begged his mother to leave.

Poor Greyson! His anxiety sure does boss him around. Sometimes anxiety is very specific. It will tell us that certain things must happen for a place to be safe. We may avoid all crowded places like movie theaters or arcades because of our anxiety, even though we really love movies and video games.

Alethia is very scared of sleepovers. She is scared that something will happen to her parents if she leaves them, but she is also scared that she will say or do something that will cause her friends to make fun of her. Her friends have sleepovers all the time and she feels so left out, but she just can't figure out how to stop her anxiety from bossing her around.

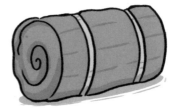

In this case, Alethia's anxiety is socially based. She is scared her friends are going to judge her. Other socially based anxieties may include talking to strangers, asking a question, presenting something, or even telling the waiter at a restaurant your order.

Now, you can start to figure out your own triggers. Use the next few exercises to see what you may be missing out on, what you're actually afraid of, and what may happen if you did what you were scared of anyway.

# What Am I Missing Out On?

As you learned from all those stories, when you let anxiety boss you around, you miss out on a ton of things. Anya doesn't get to go to her friends' houses if they have a dog, Greyson doesn't get to see a movie at a movie theater, and Alethia doesn't get to go to sleepovers. What could you be missing out on by letting your anxiety be the one in control? Next you'll find different categories: Person, Place, or Thing. List what you missed out on based upon the categories.

**Person:** Who have you not been able to spend time with or meet because of your anxiety?

-------------------------------------------------------------------------

-------------------------------------------------------------------------

**Place:** Where have you not been able to go because of your anxiety?

-------------------------------------------------------------------------

-------------------------------------------------------------------------

**Thing:** What types of things have you missed out on because of your anxiety?

-------------------------------------------------------------------------

-------------------------------------------------------------------------

# What Am I Afraid Of?

Sometimes fears and anxiety can be tricky. Remember how Alethia was scared to go to sleepovers? Well, it's not *actually* the sleepover that scares her, right? It's the anxiety about saying or doing something wrong in front of her friends. You were able to figure that out for Alethia, but what if sometimes it's not that easy? How can you figure out what you're *actually* afraid of? You can use something called a "downward arrow." You keep asking yourself certain questions until you figure out what your real fear may be and what it may mean. Let's use Alethia's fear as an example.

I'm scared of sleepovers.

**What would happen if you went to a sleepover?**

My friends may make fun of me.

**If that were true, what would that mean?**

That I'm dumb.

**What would happen next?**

They wouldn't like me.

**What would that say about you?**

That I'm not a likable person.

Using the downward arrow, you can find out that Alethia isn't actually scared of sleepovers; she is scared her friends will decide she is not a worthy friend. Soon we'll get to what Alethia can do with these thoughts; but for now, why don't you practice with your own downward arrow?

### What is the situation you are scared of?

----------------------------------------------------------------

### If it were true, what would that mean?

----------------------------------------------------------------

### What would happen next?

----------------------------------------------------------------

### What would that say about you?

----------------------------------------------------------------

# What Would Happen If I Went Anyway?

Now that you know how to find out exactly what you're scared of or anxious about, you can start to imagine what it would be like if you stopped avoiding it. This is similar to your brave activities but you're not *actually* going to face your fears; you're going to *imagine* what it would be like if you stopped avoiding them. In the thought bubbles, draw a mixture of things you could imagine happening (positive and negative) if you were to stop avoiding what you are scared of.

# WHAT IS YOUR ANXIETY TELLING YOU?

You know that anxiety has a lot to tell you at home and that it has even more to tell you at school. Now let's figure out what your anxiety is trying to tell you when you're out and about. Anxiety doesn't take a break from bossing you around; it can be bossy at home, at school, and anywhere else! Let's learn about possible triggers that may happen when you're out in the world. We'll start with an example.

Jin loves to spend time with her friends. Many weekends she will have a playdate with several of her friends at one of their houses. One Saturday, as Jin is getting ready to go to her friend Layla's house, she begins to feel nervous about what to wear. Some of her friends made fun of another girl in their class who had on a turtleneck sweater; Jin doesn't want to wear anything that may make her friends tease her. She tries on many outfits until her mom is yelling that they have to go. Jin feels nervous the whole car ride, and once they get to Layla's house, she feels like she may explode from her anxiety. When a few of the girls start laughing, Jin thinks they are making fun of her and feels so anxious that she starts crying and asks to go home.

What do you think Jin's triggers were? One of them would be trying to know exactly what her friends may or may not like. When Jin tries to read her friends' minds or always make the "right" choice, she sets herself up to be anxious because there's no way she can read someone's mind or always know what opinion someone else may have. Another trigger was when her friends started laughing and she didn't know what it was about. If Jin was able to remember that these things were her triggers and became more aware of them, maybe she wouldn't have gotten so anxious.

Let's look at a different example so you can learn more about how your thoughts about different situations can change how you feel.

Otto loves to go to museums, but recently he has been afraid to go places where a lot of strangers have been. Otto is particularly scared he is going to get other people's germs all over him, which will make him sick. He thinks about telling his parents he doesn't want to go to the museum anymore.

Now that you're an expert, you can see right away that it isn't the museum that makes Otto anxious, but his thoughts about the museum. If Otto thinks "If I go to this museum, I'll get sick, and if I get sick I won't be able to handle how awful it will be," he would likely feel very anxious. But what if Otto thinks "It's *possible* I may get sick at the museum, but it's *probable* that I won't. If I do get sick, I'll be able to handle it because I've handled it in the past, even if it was no fun"? Can you see how Otto's thoughts can completely change the way he feels about the situation?

Let's practice what you've learned. You're going to do more hypothesis testing, learn more about probable and possible situations, and create a STOP plan for when you're out and about.

# Hypothesis Testing

Let's put hypothesis testing to work, but this time we'll focus on anxieties that happen when you're out and about. First, here's a refresher on the step-by-step process of hypothesis testing:

1.  **Ask a question.**

2.  **Find out as much information about the question as you can.**

3.  **Identify your hypothesis (your guess at the answer to the question).**

4.  **Test the hypothesis.**

5.  **Look at the results of the experiment and come up with your answer (was your question right or wrong?).**

Okay, let's get started!

1.  **Question:** _____

_____

_____

2.  **Information:** _____

_____

_____

3.  **Hypothesis:** _____

_____

_____

**Hypothesis Testing,** *continued*

4.   **Test:**

5.   **Results:**

# Possible Versus Probable

You're an expert at figuring out if a situation is *possible* or *probable* at home and at school, but what about when you're out in the world? Let's identify a list of worries you have when you're out and then categorize them as possible or probable. First, here's a refresher on the definition of possible and probable:

**Possible:** Something that is *able* to be done. Something that *may* happen.

**Probable:** Something that is *likely* to be done. Something that has a better chance of happening than not happening.

Now come up with your list of worries you may have when you're out:

1. _____

2. _____

3. _____

4. _____

5. _____

Write your worries in the right category: Possible or Probable.

| POSSIBLE | PROBABLE |
|---|---|
| | |
| | |
| | |
| | |

# STOP Plan: Out in the World

This time, you'll fill out your STOP plan with something that has to do with being out in the world. It can be about performance, related to social situations, or be something specific. First, here's a refresher on the STOP plan:

**S**ITUATIONS AND TRIGGERS

**T**HOUGHTS AND FEELINGS

**O**THER WAYS TO THINK

**P**LAN OF ACTION TOWARD CHANGE

Now, fill out your very own out-in-the-world STOP plan.

| S | |
|---|---|
| **T** | |
| **O** | |
| **P** | |

# LET'S TRY SOMETHING NEW

 You know all about choice now, right? You learned that even though sometimes it feels like you don't have a choice about how you feel or behave or think, that is definitely not true. Let's focus on your behaviors whenever you're out and about. First, let's read about Roman and how his behaviors when he was out affected how he felt.

Roman loves his parents so much. He becomes very anxious when he is away from them. He really enjoys going to restaurants and hanging out with his friends, but he has been avoiding these things because that would mean leaving his parents. Roman's parents tell him that his aunt will be taking him out to dinner and the bowling alley this weekend while his parents go on a date. Roman immediately feels very anxious even though he loves his aunt, bowling, and going out to dinner. He begins to cry and scream. He begs his parents not to go on a date.

Can you see how Roman's anxiety is bossing him around? He feels so anxious being away from his parents that he would miss out on things he usually loves to do. What could Roman do differently? He could remember that his thoughts can change his feelings, which would also change his behaviors. He could tell himself he will only be away from his parents for a few hours, remind himself how much he loves bowling, and do some belly breathing to calm himself down. Roman sure would feel better if he thought that way, right? Remember, the situation didn't change. The only thing that changed was how Roman thought, behaved, and felt.

Now let's figure out some alternative positive behaviors and then make a plan for when you're out and about.

95

# Alternative Behaviors

You know what an alternative behavior is, but you may not know exactly which behaviors out in the world may be negative, and how to replace them with positive ones. Let's define some negative behaviors that usually help anxiety stick around.

1. **Avoidance (avoiding restaurants, bowling alleys, etc.)**
2. **Ignoring friends**
3. **Yelling**
4. **Fighting**
5. **Refusing to go out anywhere**

Think of a few negative behaviors you may do when you're out, and write them down.

1. _____
2. _____
3. _____
4. _____
5. _____

Now let's define some *positive* behaviors.

1. **Talking it out with your mom or dad**
2. **Taking some deep breaths**
3. **Facing your fears/doing brave activities**
4. **Asking for help**
5. **Using a coping skill**

Think of a few positive behaviors you can do while you're out and write them down.

1. _____
2. _____
3. _____
4. _____
5. _____

# Rating Our Behaviors

Remember, before you can make a plan for using your positive alternative behaviors, you need to set yourself up to succeed. In the table, assign the alternative behaviors you just defined to the Easy, Medium, or Hard columns.

| EASY ALTERNATIVE BEHAVIORS | MEDIUM ALTERNATIVE BEHAVIORS | HARD ALTERNATIVE BEHAVIORS |
|---|---|---|
|  |  |  |
|  |  |  |
|  |  |  |
|  |  |  |
|  |  |  |
|  |  |  |

# Making a Plan

Now, you can make a plan so you'll know exactly what to do when you notice you're falling into a negative behavior pattern. This activity is just like your trigger activity, except instead of just identifying triggers, you're also going to identify an alternative positive behavior you can act out.

Whenever _____ happens,
(situation or event)

I feel _____, which can then lead to
(emotion)

_____. I plan to stop this negative
(a negative behavior)

behavior by replacing it with _____.
(a positive behavior)

Whenever _____ happens,
(situation or event)

I feel _____, which can then lead to
(emotion)

_____. I plan to stop this negative
(a negative behavior)

behavior by replacing it with _____.
(a positive behavior)

Whenever _____ happens,
(situation or event)

I feel _____, which can then lead to
(emotion)

_____. I plan to stop this negative
(a negative behavior)

behavior by replacing it with _____.
(a positive behavior)

# Facing the Things That Scare You Out in the World

It's time to practice some of your acceptance strategies and gear up for brave activities! This time, let's focus your acceptance strategies on situations you may find yourself in when you're out in the world.

- **Let your feelings happen.** It's okay to feel scared because you're about to go somewhere you've never been before. It's perfectly normal to feel nervous when going to a new place, since you don't really know what to expect. When you start to judge yourself negatively (for example, thinking "If I were a better person, I wouldn't be scared right now"), you feel worse, and it certainly doesn't make your fear go away.

- **Focus on your strengths.** Remember that if you get anxious about one thing out in the world, there are plenty of things that you feel comfortable doing. Maybe you're nervous about going to a new place, but you feel comfortable being around new people. Maybe you really dislike being in a crowd, but you really enjoy spending one-on-one time with friends outside of your home. You always have strengths you can focus on, and just because you may be in the middle of something scary, doesn't mean those strengths stop existing!

- **Allow yourself to have weaknesses.** You've already learned that *everyone* has weaknesses, just like everyone has strengths! If you keep negatively judging yourself or expecting to control or get rid of every single weakness you have, you'll constantly feel anxious.

- **Don't try to be perfect.** It's still true when you're out in the world: No one is perfect. Always trying to do the impossible (like being perfect) means always being filled with disappointment, sadness, and anxiety. Give up trying to be the impossible perfect!

- **Allow difficulty to happen without trying to avoid or escape it.** There will be times out in the world when you'll feel discomfort; it's unavoidable. You may dislike crowds, but at some point, they are unavoidable. Allowing something difficult to happen helps you increase the amount of frustration you can deal with. This is known as "frustration tolerance."

- **Understand that you are *always* in control of how you respond to things, even if you don't have control over a specific situation.** You may need to go somewhere new. You may have to be in a crowded place. You may need to meet new people. You may need to do things you really don't want to do. That's life! Sometimes life is great and sometimes life is tough. It's important to remember that even when you must do something you really don't want to do, you're still always in control of your thoughts, which directly affects your feelings. You have more control than you think you do.

Now, let's gear up to complete some brave activities. Remember to grab a parent or other grown-up for this part. Here are the steps for completing brave activities:

**Step 1:** Identify what you're scared of out in the world.

**Step 2:** Figure out when you're going to do your brave activity.

**Step 3:** Identify how to calm down when the scary thing becomes too scary.

Use the next few exercises to detail your own brave activity plan.

# Brave Activity Plan: Places

Make sure you have your grown-up helper with you while you're creating and doing your brave activity plan. For this plan, you're going to focus on places that make you feel anxious or scared. Start with the least scary thing (1) and work your way up to the scariest thing (10).

| | FEER<br>What scares you? | BRAVE ACTIVITY<br>How are you going to face your fear? | WHEN<br>When do you plan to do your brave activity? | COPING<br>What skills can you use to help calm yourself down? |
|---|---|---|---|---|
| 1 | | | | |
| 2 | | | | |
| 3 | | | | |
| 4 | | | | |
| 5 | | | | |

### Brave Activity Plan: Places, *continued*

| | FEAR | BRAVE ACTIVITY | WHEN | COPING |
|---|---|---|---|---|
| 6 | | | | |
| 7 | | | | |
| 8 | | | | |
| 9 | | | | |
| 10 | | | | |

# Brave Activity Plan: People

Make sure you have your grown-up helper with you while you're creating and doing your brave activity plan. For this plan, you're going to focus on things to do with people that make you feel anxious or scared. That may be meeting someone new, talking to a stranger (like a waiter), or asking for help. Start with the least scary thing (1) and work your way up to the scariest thing (10).

| | FEAR<br>What scares you? | BRAVE ACTIVITY<br>How are you going to face your fear? | WHEN<br>When do you plan to do your brave activity? | COPING<br>What skills can you use to help calm yourself down? |
|---|---|---|---|---|
| 1 | | | | |
| 2 | | | | |
| 3 | | | | |
| 4 | | | | |
| 5 | | | | |

## Brave Activity Plan: People, *continued*

| | FEAR | BRAVE ACTIVITY | WHEN | COPING |
|---|---|---|---|---|
| 6 | | | | |
| 7 | | | | |
| 8 | | | | |
| 9 | | | | |
| 10 | | | | |

# Brave Activity Plan: Things

Make sure you have your grown-up helper with you while you're creating and doing your brave activity plan. For this plan, you're going to focus on things that make you feel anxious or scared. Things may include specific phobias (like dogs or bugs), specific objects, germs, or anything else that isn't a person or a place. Start with the least scary thing (1) and work your way up to the scariest thing (10).

| | FEAR<br>What scares you? | BRAVE ACTIVITY<br>How are you going to face your fear? | WHEN<br>When do you plan to do your brave activity? | COPING<br>What skills can you use to help calm yourself down? |
|---|---|---|---|---|
| 1 | | | | |
| 2 | | | | |
| 3 | | | | |
| 4 | | | | |
| 5 | | | | |

## Brave Activity Plan: Things, *continued*

| | FEAR | BRAVE ACTIVITY | WHEN | COPING |
|---|---|---|---|---|
| 6 | | | | |
| 7 | | | | |
| 8 | | | | |
| 9 | | | | |
| 10 | | | | |

# YOU DID IT!

You've worked so hard and learned so many things about your anxiety and what you can do about it. Now you know more about your anxiety: when, how, and why you get anxious, and different things you can do to feel better—at home, at school, and out in the world. You've also learned how your thoughts, feelings, and behaviors all act together and how much more control you have than you probably realized. I know it couldn't have been easy—you faced things you were really scared of and you used all your cool new coping tools to make it through.

You truly deserve huge congratulations. Celebrate your big accomplishment! Whether you completed one, two, or all the activities in this book, you are one brave kid. The most important thing to remember is that it's okay if one day you feel anxiety again. Remember, anxiety can sometimes be helpful, and it certainly is something we cannot completely avoid feeling. Take it one day at a time, and remember to use your coping tools if anxiety ever tries to boss you around again!

# JUST FOR PARENTS

# ARE YOU FEEDING YOUR CHILD'S ANXIETY?

Being a parent can be one of life's most rewarding and wonderful experiences, but it can also be extremely difficult, and it definitely doesn't come with an instruction manual. If you have a child struggling with anxiety, it can feel overwhelming and frightening for you as a parent, as well.

Most parents would agree that they want what's best for their child, but what exactly is the best response to your child's anxiety? When your child is in distress—frightened, crying—a parent's first instinct is likely to offer comfort and reassurance. However, when you're dealing with an anxious child, reassuring them fuels their anxiety rather than soothing it. An anxious child will feed off your reassurance to the point that they believe they must receive a steady stream of it in order to stay safe. This happens for a number of reasons:

- Reassurance validates the anxiety by reinforcing your child's irrational belief that they're in danger.

- It encourages your child to avoid things that scare them by reinforcing the idea that they need protection.

- It acts as a form of *negative reinforcement* by temporarily reducing your child's anxiety, therefore increasing the likelihood that they will seek more and more reassurance from you in the future.

- It can be harmful to your family dynamic and put a strain on the child/ parent relationship.

Constant reassuring, rescuing, or protecting can also stunt the development of your child's distress tolerance. Distress tolerance is human beings' way of dealing with negative and difficult situations. The more you experience something, like a difficult situation, the more tolerance for it you gain. Unpleasant or even painful experiences are an inevitable part of life, so learning to tolerate uncomfortable feelings is an important part of your child's healthy development. But if, when your child encounters difficulties, you swoop in to lower their distress with reassurance, their ability to deal with ups and downs will decrease. Over time, they will become less and less willing to face situations that trigger their anxiety.

There are other ways parents can inadvertently enable their kids' anxiety. As we've seen, a parent can enable their child's anxiety simply by reassuring them that everything will be okay. This may be 100 percent true, but if you consistently reassure your child this way, they are able to avoid the unknown and therefore lose the opportunity to increase distress tolerance. A parent can also enable their child's anxiety by removing them from the stressful situation. Complete removal of stress reinforces avoidant behaviors and also lowers distress tolerance. A parent can enable their child's anxiety by telling them exactly what to do about their anxiety. If a child believes their parent will tell them what to do, it lowers their need for cognitive exploration and stunts cognitive growth, flexibility, confidence, and the child's sense of personal agency.

However, as a parent, you don't want to completely ignore your child's distress, so it can be a tricky balancing act. How can you be supportive without inadvertently feeding your child's anxiety? One way is by talking through the problem with them. Providing your child with the opportunity to explore their thoughts and emotions without necessarily reassuring them can increase distress tolerance and self-confidence. Another way is by helping them identify coping strategies they can use in a stressful situation. You don't need to remove them or tell them exactly what to do, but you absolutely can remind them about coping strategies they've learned, or ask them which of several tactics might work best given the situation and how they're feeling. This facilitates cognitive growth, independence, and self-confidence, which can help lower anxiety.

You've already taken a huge step toward helping your anxious child by purchasing this book and reading this special section for parents. Remember, exposing your child to the things that make them anxious can also be scary for you, so at first you might feel a bit uneasy with these new tactics. But all the research shows this is the best way to help your child learn to manage their anxiety and keep moving toward a happy, healthy life.

Now, let's look at some specific things you can do to stop reinforcing your child's anxiety and start helping them learn to manage it.

# Does Your Child Need More Support?

At what point does my child's anxiety indicate a need for professional help? What does professional help look like? Won't my child be stigmatized if I get them professional help?

These and a million other questions may be swirling throughout your head. You and your child may follow all the strategies in this book, complete all the activities, and succeed in introducing the basic concepts of cognitive behavioral therapy to your lives, and in the end, you may still feel you're at the mercy of your child's anxiety. So, when is it time to get help?

It really comes down to your child's level of distress and functioning. Are they refusing school, failing classes, in distress more often throughout the day than they are *not* in distress? If you answered yes to any of those questions, it may be time to get outside support. Many parents fear they'll be viewed as a failure if they seek professional help, but in fact it takes strength and courage to acknowledge when you need support. A therapist's goal is not to "fix" your child, but to teach a parent, a child, and the family unit the best way to overcome a problem by working together. If you feel your family would benefit from professional support, search online for licensed therapists in your community, or ask your medical provider how to get a referral.

# STOP REINFORCING AVOIDANCE & SAFETY SEEKING

The idea of stopping your enabling behaviors, providing new supports, and facilitating your child's exposure to anxiety-provoking events may feel overwhelming. As a parent, you have a lot going on. You may have a full-time job, other children, and your own difficulties and challenges. It can seem easier in the moment to soothe your child by telling them they're fine or that everything is going to be okay. It may seem easier in the moment to let your child avoid something or handle the problem yourself. But the short-term fix perpetuates the long-term problem. The best solution is to find a strategy that works for your individual family. You don't need to rush your child; small steps can create big changes, if you stick with the strategies and keep practicing. Every time your child practices a new anxiety-management skill or faces a scary situation, their new, more adaptive behaviors will be reinforced, which is the key to maintaining their gains.

Let's see what this looks like in action. We'll use bedtime (a common challenge for many families) as an example of how important reinforcement is. Say your child cries and begs to sleep in your bed because they're afraid of the dark. Every time you allow it, you have inadvertently *reinforced* the begging and crying—meaning you've increased the likelihood of your child doing it again in the future. To you, it might feel like you're just being supportive of your scared child, but when one night turns into five in a row, you might realize that you—and your child—have walked into a trap.

You're five nights in and you want your kid to go back to their own bed, but their anxiety seems higher than ever. Now, in order to get your child to return to their bed, you repeatedly reassure them that they'll be okay and nothing will happen to them. In response to their repeated questions "Will I be safe?" you reassure them again and again, from dinnertime until bedtime. Exhausting, right? And to top it off, you're still reinforcing their anxiety through what psychologists call *safety seeking*.

Safety seeking is a cluster of coping behaviors used to reduce anxiety. Seeking parental reassurance—like repeatedly asking you to tell them they'll be safe—is a form of safety seeking. Other examples include a child with a social anxiety, who may run through a litany of questions—*Will there be cake? What happens if it rains? What time will you pick me up?*—before they're willing to get in the car and go to a birthday party. A child with germ or contamination anxiety may wear gloves as their safety-seeking behavior. A child with OCD might compulsively wash their hands or count all the tiles in the ceiling. These are all behaviors that make your child feel less anxious in the short term but will disrupt their lives and increase their anxiety over time.

As a parent, you just can't win every fight. You'll accidentally reinforce problem behaviors, you'll sometimes say the wrong thing, or you'll occasionally choose the quick way through a problem instead of the best way. It's natural. What you want to focus on now is reframing the way you respond to your anxious child in order to facilitate their development of independence, self-esteem, distress tolerance, and flexibility. To do this, you'll need to work on your communication techniques, boundary setting, and the consistent use of consequences to reduce problematic behaviors and increase desired behaviors.

Use the next few pages to identify ways you may be reinforcing your child's avoidance and safety-seeking behaviors, and how you can start to reinforce positive behaviors and move toward reducing their anxiety.

# COMMON PARENT BEHAVIORS

The first step toward change is identification. In the table you'll find a list of common parent avoidant and safety behaviors. Circle the ones that fit you. The rest of the columns are blank for you to fill in your specific avoidance and safety behaviors.

| AVOIDANCE | SAFETY |
|---|---|
| **Avoiding tantrums.** This may include giving in to your child's demands by providing them with the reassurance they want or letting them avoid what scares them. | **Planning around your child's fear** instead of exposing them to it. This may include driving a child to school every day because they're anxious about riding the school bus. |
| **Avoiding fights.** You may avoid fights by giving in to your child's demands, reassuring them, or avoiding the problem yourself. | **Providing reassurance** that your child will be okay, that there isn't anything to fear, or something similar. |
| **Avoiding negative emotions.** Instead of allowing yourself or your child to feel frustrated, angry, or scared, you may avoid the situation or give in to the demands. | **Giving in to your child's demands** whether that be a demand to avoid something, a demand for reassurance, or another demand. |
| **Avoiding creating and implementing a strict set of rules and expectations.** You may avoid punishment or rules in order to "keep the peace" in the house. | **Facilitating your child's negative safety-seeking behaviors.** This can include helping them engage in specific irrational behaviors that decrease their anxiety, such as individually wrapping your child's food due to their fear of contamination. |

| AVOIDANCE | SAFETY |
|---|---|
|  |  |
|  |  |
|  |  |
|  |  |

# PARENT ACTION PLAN

A point system for your child that your family can use is an excellent way to hold yourself accountable as a parent and also reinforce your child's positive behaviors. The more specific and identifiable the expectations, the less anxious your child feels. For every behavior they accomplish, they get a point that can be traded in at the end of the week or the month. You can come up with whatever reinforcers you think will fit you and your child best. Some parents may choose things like:

1. **A special dessert**
2. **A special toy**
3. **Mom and me or Dad and me day**
4. **Fifteen minutes extra screen time**

If you tend to avoid your child's tantrums by letting them sleep in your bed, avoid going to school, stay home from a birthday party, etc., you'll want to identify what the positive alternative behavior would be—such as agreeing to go to the party, or to a friend's house for just an hour—and reinforce it every time it occurs. You want to set your child up to succeed so they gain more self-esteem and independence, which can dramatically reduce anxiety. Come up with two to four behaviors to focus on, making sure that a couple of them are fairly easy to accomplish.

Following are some charts to help you create your action plan. You'll take the avoidant/safety behaviors you identified and come up with ways to extinguish those behaviors by reinforcing alternative/positive behaviors.

Here's an example. On the next page you'll find a blank one for you to create your own. Remember, each day the child completes the expected task they receive one point. At the end of each week, the child can trade in their points for reinforcers.

| | SLEEPS IN OWN BED | COMPLETES CHORE OF THE DAY | GETS TO SCHOOL ON TIME | COMPLETES BRAVE ACTIVITY |
|---|---|---|---|---|
| Monday | | | | |
| Tuesday | | | | |
| Wednesday | | | | |
| Thursday | | | | |
| Friday | | | | |
| Saturday | | | | |
| Sunday | | | | |

# MANAGING YOUR OWN ANXIETY

The power of parental empathy means that you feel what your child feels. When your child starts to feel anxious, your anxiety may spike, too. As parents, we hold ourselves to unrealistic standards, expecting that we can somehow ignore our own emotions and challenges and focus only on our child. The problem with this expectation is that it dismisses your own emotional experience as a parent and also overlooks the very real fact that when you're anxious, overwhelmed, and exhausted, it affects how you interact with your child.

Anxiety is cyclical; it feeds off itself. When your child feels anxious, which triggers *your* anxiety, it can cause a negative feedback loop. An anxious parent may be more irritable or hypervigilant, which children can easily pick up on. A parent's anxiety reinforces the idea that there is something to be anxious about, so the child's anxiety grows. This creates a loop where the actual cause of the anxiety is lost and both parent and child feed off each other negatively, increasing feelings of hopelessness and exhaustion. When a child is exhausted, they are less able to deal with distress, and when a parent is exhausted, they have less patience and energy to deal effectively with challenges.

It may seem impossible to keep your cool when your child is in the midst of intense anxiety. But a calm parent will strengthen their child's chances of overcoming their anxiety spike. There are many ways to manage your own anxiety, and they vary from basic coping strategies to cognitive challenging. A basic coping strategy is something you can use in a moment of stress or anxiety in order to calm down. Here are several common coping strategies that have proven effective in reducing anxiety:

| | | |
|---|---|---|
| READING A BOOK | GOING FOR A SWIM | WATCHING A MOVIE |
| ABDOMINAL BREATHING | TAKING A BATH | YOGA |
| ENGAGING IN SELF-CARE | DRAWING | WORKING OUT |
| TAKING A WALK | JOURNALING | GOING FOR A RUN |
| GUIDED MEDITATION | TALKING IT OUT | ALONE TIME |

Coping strategies facilitate calm and well-being, which reduces stress and anxiety. However, they don't solve underlying problems; they are simply tools you can use to stay calm when problems arise. To address the problems themselves, you will have to take a closer look at what kinds of emotions and beliefs are triggering the behaviors that hold you back from helping your child more effectively.

Let's take a closer look at what I mean by that. Many people are under the impression that their emotions are a direct consequence of their experiences or the situations they find themselves in. For example, if you get fired from your job you may directly relate that to why you feel anxious and depressed. The reality is that it is your perception of the situation that changes how you feel. If you think that the job you just lost defines your worth, feeling anxious and depressed makes sense. If you perceive the job you just lost as another hurdle in life but nothing self-defining, you will likely feel some concern or sadness but certainly not severe anxiety or depression. The situation is the same—you still lost your job—but how you feel is entirely based upon how you perceive the situation. Similarly, how you perceive your ability to both change your behavior and help your child change theirs will directly impact how well your whole family learns to manage your child's anxiety symptoms.

The next few exercises can help you solidify positive coping strategies and practice your own cognitive skills, so you can not only be the best parent to your anxious child, but also feel better overall and move toward a happier and healthier family unit.

# Guided Meditation

Studies have shown meditation practices can significantly decrease stress and anxiety. Guided meditation is a type of meditation where you are softly guided through a scenario in order to facilitate mindfulness and become more aware of your physical responses to aid in the reduction of tension and stress. What follows is an example of a guided meditation script that takes five to ten minutes.

Let's start by focusing on the breath. Take a minute to focus on how you're breathing. Notice what it feels like to breathe in and breathe out. Feel your stomach and chest moving in synchronicity. Feel your lungs expand and deflate, expand and deflate. Close your eyes and continue focusing on your natural breathing rate for the next few minutes.

Now let's focus on controlling our breathing rate. Take a deep inhale counting 1, 2, 3, 4, then hold the breath for 1, 2, and now exhale counting 1, 2, 3, 4, 5. Continue with this focused breathing rate for the next few minutes. It's perfectly fine if at some moment you find your mind wandering. Gently bring your thoughts back to your breath when this happens.

Let's bring more awareness to each controlled breath you take. As you inhale, notice what it feels like in your nostrils, in your stomach, in your lungs. Feel the air pass through your nose, down your throat, and into your lungs. Now turn your attention to the transition period between inhale and exhale. Focus on creating smooth transitions and what that smooth transition feels like each time. Move on to the air coming up and out of your lungs and the next transition.

Slowly return your breathing to a less controlled state. Continue to focus on your breath, but stop counting and controlling the pause between inhales and exhales. Continue this with your eyes closed for a few minutes. Upon completion, give yourself another few minutes to adjust to your environment and then return to your daily tasks.

# Cognitive Challenging: The Thought Log

A thought log is a tool you can use to analyze your own thought process, challenge negative and irrational thoughts, and identify alternative perspectives in order to reduce negative emotions. You'll learn how to think more rationally about certain negative instances and keep your own emotions in check.

Use each column to write about a specific situation that caused a negative emotion. Keep in mind that you need to use a *fact* for the evidence that supports or goes against an unhelpful thought; it can be easy to confuse feelings with facts.

| | |
|---|---|
| **SITUATION/TRIGGER: WHAT HAPPENED?** (e.g., My child won't sleep in their own bed) | |
| **EMOTIONS/PHYSICAL SENSATIONS EXPERIENCED** (e.g., sadness, anxiety, headache, etc.) | |
| **UNHELPFUL THOUGHTS** (e.g., I'm failing as a parent) | |
| **EVIDENCE SUPPORTING THE UNHELPFUL THOUGHT** (must be a fact) | |
| **EVIDENCE THAT GOES AGAINST THE UNHELPFUL THOUGHT** (must be a fact) | |
| **ALTERNATIVE PERSPECTIVE** (e.g., My child's struggles are not indicative of my worth as a parent) | |

# Cognitive Distortions

Cognitive distortions are inaccurate thoughts that reinforce negative thought patterns or emotions. Some common distortions are listed, with space for you to provide an example of when you used that specific cognitive distortion.

## POLARIZED THINKING

When you see things as black and white, with no grey area. Perfectionistic thoughts are usually polarized, or thoughts that include *always* or *never*.

-------------------------------------------------------------------

-------------------------------------------------------------------

## OVERGENERALIZATION

When you take one incident, situation, or point in time as the sole piece of evidence for a general conclusion.

-------------------------------------------------------------------

-------------------------------------------------------------------

## CATASTROPHIZING

When you expect the worst will happen or has happened, based on an incident that is not as horrible as it was made out to be.

-------------------------------------------------------------------

-------------------------------------------------------------------

## PERSONALIZATION

When you place so much power upon yourself, you believe anything you do will have significant impacts or ramifications on other people.

-------------------------------------------------------------------------

-------------------------------------------------------------------------

## SHOULD STATEMENTS

When you place rules on yourself about how you and other people should behave: "I should have gotten that job." "I should always know how to soothe my child."

-------------------------------------------------------------------------

-------------------------------------------------------------------------

Take a deep breath and remind yourself that you're doing the very best you can. Being a parent is hard, and it's even harder when you have a child struggling with anxiety. It's not easy to admit there's a problem, and it's not easy to do the work needed to change. You're learning new strategies that your child can implement, but you're also learning new strategies you can use yourself. Remember—your own behavior is an important part of this equation, and I hope this book will arm you with a different perspective and the resources you need to move your family forward in a positive way.

# BOOKS

***Coping Cat Workbook* by Philip C. Kendall, PhD, ABPP and Kristina A. Hedtke, MA. Ardmore, PA: Workbook Publishing, 2006.**

Coping Cat is a cognitive-behavioral treatment for children with anxiety. The program helps children better understand their emotions, identify physical reactions to stress and anxiety, clarify thoughts and feelings in anxious situations, develop a plan for effective coping, and evaluate performance for self-reinforcement.

***Parent Management Training* by Dr. Alan E. Kazdin. New York: Oxford University Press, 2008.**

Parent management training (PMT) is an evidence-based therapy that teaches parents how to respond to their child in order to stop negative behaviors and reinforce positive behaviors.

# WEBSITES

**Biofeedback/Neurofeedback: www.bcia.org**

Biofeedback is a type of evidence-based therapy for children with anxiety. It focuses on the mind-body connection and teaches a child how to take control of their physical state. The website provides a detailed description of the therapy along with a search bar to find therapists in your area.

**Parent-Child Interaction Therapy: www.pcit.org**

Parent-Child Interaction Therapy (PCIT) is a type of evidence-based therapy for young children with behavioral problems. The therapist can view and coach the parent in live sessions through an observation room with a one-way mirror. The website provides a detailed description of the therapy along with a search bar to find therapists in your area.

**Psychology Today: www.psychologytoday.com**

Psychology Today is a website that contains a verified list of psychologists, psychiatrists, mental health counselors, and social workers in your specific area. You can search for specific types of treatments (individual, group, couples) and areas of expertise (child psychologists, trauma focused, etc.). They also publish articles about popular topics in the current literature.

**Trauma-Focused Cognitive Behavioral Therapy: www.tfcbt.org**

Trauma-focused cognitive behavioral therapy (TF-CBT) is a type of evidence-based therapy that focuses directly on trauma and how it is impacting a child's life. The website provides a detailed description of the process along with a search bar to find a therapist in your area that specializes in TF-CBT.

# Index

# Acknowledgments

• • • • • • • • • • • • • • • • • • • • • • • • • • • • • • •

My sincerest gratitude goes out to everyone that played a role in the creation of this workbook. First, my mother, who supported every personal, academic, and professional pursuit I identified. Without her, I would not be where I am today. Second, my husband Robb, who has sacrificed so much for me to succeed and who provided me with complete and unconditional love throughout the process. Third, my publisher Callisto, and editor, Camille Hayes, for giving me the opportunity to write down my practices and share my passion. Last, but certainly not least, I want to thank all the children and families I have worked with in the past and all of those that I will work with in the future: You are the ones that maintain my hope and passion.

# About the Author

**Dr. Heather Davidson** is a New York State–licensed child psychologist and board-certified neurotherapist. Currently, she is the director of child and adolescent services and the director of clinical training at a practice in Manhattan. Working with and helping children is one of Dr. Davidson's greatest joys.

Dr. Davidson received her bachelor's degree in psychology from West Virginia University and her master's and doctoral degrees from the Chicago School of Professional Psychology. She holds certifications from Columbia University in suicide assessment and the Albert Ellis Institute in cognitive behavioral therapy (CBT) and rational emotive behavior therapy (REBT).

Previous to her practice in New York, Dr. Davidson worked in psychiatric hospitals and community mental health facilities; she spent time in a Peruvian medical orphanage using psychiatric interventions with the children and creating and implementing a psychiatric training program.

Dr. Davidson is an avid member of the neurotherapy community. She is one of the youngest speakers at several annual international conferences and regularly speaks at schools throughout Manhattan, including Columbia University. She has made several media appearances demonstrating neurological changes based upon psychological symptoms.